I dedicate this book to Michael, my mom, and my dad's loving memory —R. G.

To my father, who taught his children that cooking is a fine art —S. P.

Published by Bloomsbury Publishing, New York, London, and Berlin
Distributed to the trade by Holtzbrinck Publishers

Library of Congress Cataloging-in-Publication Data
Gold, Rozanne.
Kids cook 1-2-3 / by Rozanne Gold ; illustrations by Sara Pinto.—1st U.S. ed.
p.   cm.
ISBN-10: 1-58234-735-2 • ISBN-13: 978-1-58234-735-6
1. Cookery—Juvenile literature. 2. Quick and easy cookery—Juvenile literature.
I. Title: Kids cook one-two-three. II. Pinto, Sara, ill. III. Title.
TX652.5.G546 2006   641.5'123—dc22   2006000623

Book design by Sue Schlabach
First U.S. Edition 2006
Printed in China
3 5 7 9 10 8 6 4

Bloomsbury Publishing, Children's Books, U.S.A.
175 Fifth Avenue, New York, NY 10010

All papers used by Bloomsbury Publishing are natural, recyclable products made from wood
grown in well-managed forests. The manufacturing processes conform to the
evironmental regulations of the country of origin.

Note about this book:
As with almost any cookbook, this one includes recipes that require cooking with
heat and cutting with sharp implements including knives and graters. Any child in a
kitchen should be supervised by a parent or guardian. The creators of this
cookbook take no responsibility for unsupervised cooking by a child—
but have included guidelines for safer cooking.

KIDS COOK 1 - 2 - 3

Recipes for young chefs

using only **3** *ingredients*

BY ROZANNE GOLD

Illustrated by Sara Pinto

BLOOMSBURY
CHILDREN'S
BOOKS

chef's hat (not required)

Table of Contents

Introduction

MY MOTHER TOLD ME THAT when I was young, I carried a cookbook around with me like a security blanket. I was never without it. I read it in the bathroom, tucked it under my pillow, and, of course, brought it to the kitchen!

I adored watching my dad as he stirred pickle relish into the yummy tuna salad that he always made in a big wooden bowl (see page 56) and I often helped my mother prepare my favorite comfort foods, including buttered noodles with cinnamon-sugar (see page 76).

Cooking with friends was *always* fun. I had an older pal from camp named Mim who loved to bake. One day she came to my house and taught me how to make biscuits. She served them warm with homemade butter (see page 43) that came together in front of my eyes. It was amazing! When I was a little older, I made heart-shaped meat loaves, just like my mother did, and invited friends for lunch.

Later in life, I became a professional chef. I helped create some of the world's most magical restaurants and once cooked for a president and a prime minister. (Who knew where my food obsession would lead?)

Cooking always had a special place in my day . . . and in my heart. In the kitchen, there was always time for laughter, learning, and sharing.

Cooking can be as easy as 1-2-3. And it should be! Especially if you're just learning how. A kind of magic occurs when three simple ingredients are transformed into delicious, easy-to-prepare recipes. When you cook your way through this book, you will begin to feel confident in the kitchen. You'll be eager to help get dinner on the table, pack your own lunch, make breakfast in bed for your mother, or plan a holiday menu. You also might start creating three-ingredient recipes of your own.

Getting Started

Even though you might not become a professional chef, it's never too early to start thinking like one. Chefs are both disciplined *and* creative. They enjoy cooking and pleasing others.

Chefs get great satisfaction from transforming nature's best ingredients into delicious meals for friends and family to share. They follow recipes carefully so that the food is consistently good *every* time it's made. But most of all, they bring a positive attitude and a great deal of energy to the kitchen. That's where the real fun comes in!

So, get yourself a nice white apron (chef's hat not required) and let's start cooking!

Kitchen Basics

You don't need a fancy kitchen to get started. What you do need is a clean countertop on which to work, a stovetop (either gas or electric), an oven, and a broiler. A toaster oven also is helpful, especially for making quick and healthy snacks after school. You need pots and pans of various sizes (see page 16), bowls, spoons, cutting boards, and several knives, which must be handled with care (see page 17).

Food Safety

First and foremost, it is essential to **wash your hands** with soap and warm water and to make sure your work area is very clean before you start cooking. As you handle raw foods, like meat or fish or vegetables, you should wash your hands, and cutting boards, frequently.

Good chefs always **clean up** as they go along. This keeps the dirty things away from the clean things and prevents a mess from building up.

Put fresh ingredients in the **refrigerator** as soon as you purchase them and as soon as you're finished working with them. Let hot ingredients cool to room temperature before refrigerating them. Do not leave food out for longer than a recipe specifies.

Check the **expiration date** on canned and jarred ingredients. Rinse fruits and vegetables very well before using. Smell everything you use. If it smells bad, throw it out!

Personal Safety

Kitchens can be very safe places to work, if you follow some simple rules. Always wear **sturdy shoes** just in case anything falls near your feet. **Don't wear loose clothing** or wide sleeves: you don't want to get them wet, dirty, or, worst of all, burned! If you have long hair, pull it back. Never use an oven or broiler without a "kitchen buddy" (parent, older sibling, or older friend).

It's important to go slowly and concentrate. Work on only one step or procedure at a time.

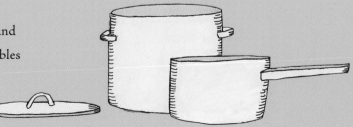

Danger Zones

Always use **pot holders** or oven mitts to touch **hot pans**. Use **knives** with care. You might use a small knife after you have gained some confidence and skill. Use large knives with adult supervision. It is important to make sure your knives are **sharp** and in good condition. Dull knives are no good for cutting and can hurt you more easily than sharp ones. When you are using a knife, angle it away from you and don't cut toward you or your fingers. Pay attention to where the edge of the blade is at all times and keep your **fingers curled and away from the blade. Do not try to catch a knife if it falls**; rather, quickly step out of the way and pick it up from the fall. Wash it carefully. Store knives on a knife rack or in a knife block.

Be sure to use the **right knife for the right job**: see page 17 for types of knives needed. Always use a **cutting board**: To keep it firmly in place, put a damp kitchen towel or a shallow stack of paper towels underneath.

Water

Fill pots two-thirds full, otherwise they will overflow while you cook, causing burns and making a mess. Be sure to follow the rules of a recipe when it specifies to simmer (small bubbles, low heat), cook over medium heat, or bring to a boil.

Electricity

Always keep electric appliances away from the sink and any water. Make certain to turn off all electric appliances and sources of heat (oven, stove, etc.) as soon as you finish.

Practice cooking skills and techniques with your **kitchen buddy**. If a recipe says to make sure you "do this with an adult," make sure you do. Let them show you how to use the blender, food processor, electric mixer, or can opener with care.

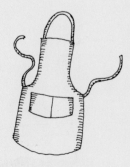

About the Recipes

The recipes in *Kids Cook 1-2-3* were created by me and then tested by a team of young sous-chefs (assistant chefs). They are Danielle Hartog, age 11; Robyn Kimmel, age 8; Ian Kimmel, age 12; Daniel Glass, age 11; Sara Rosen, age 16; Benjamin Deem, age 10; Max Deem, age 12; Rachel Greenberg, age 12; Daniel Greenberg, age 10; Phillip L. Safran, age 10; Nicholas Green, age 11; Sara Feld, age 15; and Julia Miller, age 11. Their feedback and enthusiasm were invaluable to me in choosing which recipes to include.

The Magic of 1-2-3

When it comes to cooking, three is a magical number. I have found that three ingredients of uncompromising quality often are all you need to create dishes that taste more delicious than the sum of their parts. The expression "less is more" works surprisingly well in the culinary arts. Sometimes recipes have *sooo* many ingredients that they become overwhelming. My 1-2-3 approach is especially appropriate for younger cooks and budding gourmets who like simple foods and balanced flavors. Keeping it simple also means you can really focus on what you're doing; it makes cooking more user-friendly, without taking any shortcuts. Three ingredients also means less shopping, less preparation, and less cleanup, too!

Most magical of all is watching a chocolate cake evolve from a mere trio of ingredients—eggs, chocolate, and butter—or an entire meal from just twelve ingredients. No wonder my young sous-chefs had so much fun testing the recipes!

Flavor and Taste

There are no rights or wrongs in the way we experience taste. Our taste buds are as individual as our fingerprints, and I encourage you to figure out for yourself the flavors and dishes you like. And remember this: **Your tastes change as you grow older**; something that you dislike today might become your favorite food next year!

When we eat food, we bring all our senses to the table: sight, smell, taste, touch, and even sound (think of the sound a potato chip makes as it goes c-r-u-n-c-h in your mouth!). Smell is a very big part of the equation: When we smell something delicious, our mouths begin to water and our hunger is stimulated. Or, when we have a cold, it is sometimes hard to taste food because our noses are clogged!

Our sense of taste is complex because it relates to different parts of our brain and autonomic nervous system. But it's fun to just think about taste as you cook your way through this book. Good foods are generally a pleasing combination of these flavors: **salty, sour, sweet, and bitter**. You might try a dish and say, "I really like this because it is salty and sweet." Or, "I don't like this because it is too sour or bitter." You might also begin to make small adjustments to my recipes to suit your own taste by adding another pinch of salt or an extra squeeze of lemon juice.

How to Follow a Recipe

It is important to read a recipe slowly and carefully all the way through before you get started. This way you will know what ingredients to buy and what utensils you will need. You will also know if you will be needing a stove or other equipment that will require a kitchen buddy to cook with.

It's a good idea to **set all your ingredients out in front of you** and prepare them according to the procedures in the recipe. In professional kitchens this is called *mise en place*, which is French for "everything in its place." It is important to measure the ingredients carefully and to follow the instructions as they are written—otherwise there is no guarantee that the recipe will turn out at all! You will find some helpful **cooking terms** at the end of this chapter.

Anytime that you are trying a recipe for the first time, or one that uses a hot stove, knives, or electrical appliances, please be sure you have a parent or kitchen buddy to help you.

Measuring

Here are a few important things to know for measuring ingredients correctly in a recipe.

Measuring spoons come in these sizes:

1/4 teaspoon; 1/2 teaspoon;

1 teaspoon; 1 tablespoon

3 teaspoons = 1 tablespoon

4 tablespoons = 1/4 cup

8 tablespoons = 1/2 cup

16 tablespoons = 1 cup

1 cup = 8 ounces liquid

4 cups = 1 quart liquid

1 pound = 16 ounces by weight

Glass or plastic pitcher-style "liquid" measuring cups (the type with a lip for pouring) are used for measuring liquids.

Metal or plastic "dry" measuring cups are used for measuring dry ingredients (such as flour or sugar).

When using measuring spoons and cups, level off the ingredients with the straight edge of a blunt knife.

The 1-2-3 Pantry

Most of the recipes in this book are based on fresh, natural ingredients. However, a well-stocked pantry—with good olive oil in your cupboard, puff pastry in your freezer, and pesto in your fridge—is essential in cooking 1-2-3.

In the Cupboard or Pantry

Olive oil, for cooking

Extra-virgin olive oil, for salads and dressings

Vegetable oil

Apple cider vinegar

White balsamic vinegar

Raspberry vinegar

Light coconut milk (Thai Kitchen brand or
   preferably one from Asia)

Sweetened condensed milk

Old-fashioned rolled oats (oatmeal)

Orange blossom honey

Spices: salt, pepper, cinnamon sticks, cumin,
   star anise, five-spice powder, black sesame
   seeds, white sesame seeds

Sugar: granulated, confectioners', dark brown,
   turbinado (raw brown)

Nutella (a chocolate–hazelnut spread)

Peanut butter

Pure maple syrup (not pancake syrup)

V-8 juice

Chocolate bars and chips: milk chocolate,
   semisweet, and white chocolate

Unsweetened cocoa powder

Cinnamon-sugar (store-bought or
   homemade)

To Make Cinnamon-Sugar:

In a small bowl, stir together 1 cup of sugar
and 1½ tablespoons ground cinnamon. Pour or
spoon the mixture into
a jar. Lasts indefinitely.
Makes 1 cup

In the Freezer

Puff pastry

Vanilla ice cream

In the Refrigerator

Pesto sauce

Mayonnaise, regular or light

Extra-large eggs

Plain yogurt

Parmesan cheese: use freshly grated Parmigiano-
   Reggiano, when possible (imported from Italy)

Ingredients

Substitutions

If you can't find any of the ingredients in a
recipe, it is best not to make that particular
recipe since I can't promise what the outcome
will be! However, you generally can substitute
whole milk for low-fat milk or large eggs
for extra-large eggs with good results. The
good news is that almost all of the ingredients
in the recipes can be found in your local
supermarket.

Salt, Pepper, and Water

These ingredients don't get counted in the
three-ingredient formula because they are
fundamental in cooking. So you will not find
them in the ingredient lists but instead will
find them in the procedures. Think of them as
the free ingredients in these recipes. Water
means tap water, or bottled or filtered water if
your environment requires it. Salt generally
means table salt, or kosher salt where specified.
Pepper generally means black pepper that is
freshly ground from a pepper mill. Sometimes
white pepper is used. I have two pepper mills:
One is filled with black peppercorns and
one is filled with white peppercorns. In some
recipes specific amounts of salt and pepper are
called for; other times it says add salt and pepper to taste, which means it is up to you.

Buying the Best

Because each recipe in this book is based on
just three carefully balanced ingredients, it is
important that you buy the best. Every chef
knows that you can't make delicious food
from inferior products. So . . . buy ingredients
in season, buy the freshest-smelling and best-
looking, and buy from reputable sources.
If you are lucky enough to have a butcher,
fishmonger, fruit stand, or local farmer's
markets, so much the better. It's fun to shop
and look for the best of everything.
Sometimes this means paying a little more,
but when you buy "in season," fruits and vegetables are generally cheaper. Get to know the
names of the people you buy from. They will
love to know that you're interested in what
they do.

Equipment

You don't need to have many pots and pans to cook the recipes in this book. I don't own a microwave oven or even a dishwasher. I love to wash dishes! I use small, medium, and large frying pans or skillets that are shallow and have slightly sloping sides. I also use a very large sauté pan with a cover. Sauté pans have straight sides and are a bit deeper than skillets.

Here's what will come in handy:

Pots and Pans

Saucepans with covers (2-quart, 3-quart, and 4-quart)

Pot with a cover (8-quart)

Pot fitted with a steamer basket

Small nonstick skillets or frying pans (7- and 8-inch)

Medium nonstick skillet or frying pan (9-inch)

Large nonstick skillet or frying pan (10-inch)

Very large nonstick sauté pan with cover (12-inch)

Wok

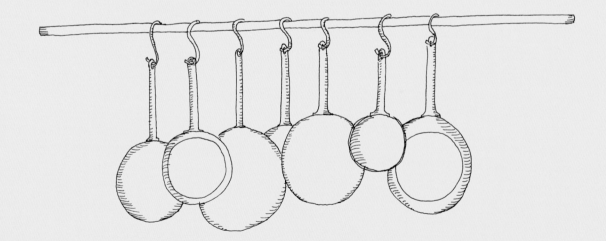

Knives

Have a **paring knife** with a blade that is between 3 and 4 inches long. A 3½-inch blade is the most common and useful. It is the "small jobs" knife, for peeling, coring, trimming (the tough outer layer of broccoli), slicing, or for mincing.

A **utility knife** with a 6-inch blade is perfect for small onions and carrots, apples and pears, and the like. You also need an all-purpose 8- or 9-inch **chef's knife** for chopping, for slicing larger fruits and vegetables, and for slicing or trimming fish and meat.

An 8-inch **serrated knife**, with its jagged blade, is best for slicing bread, tomatoes, citrus fruit, sandwiches, brownies and cakes, and any pastry with a delicate crust.

Electrical Applicances

I use a variety of appliances: a blender, a food processor, and a standing mixer with a balloon whisk and a paddle attachment. Or you may use a hand-held mixer. I often use my toaster oven, too. That's it!

Other Things You Might Need

Box grater	Microplane grater	Potato masher
Colander	Mixing bowls	Rimmed baking sheets
Cutting board	Parchment paper	Vegetable peeler
Flexible rubber spatula	Pitcher-style measuring cups for	Wire (mesh) strainer
Garlic press	liquids (usually made of glass	Wire whisks
Ice cream maker	or plastic)	Wooden spoons
(manual or electric)		
Ice cream scoop		
Measuring cups for dry		
ingredients (usually made		
of metal or plastic)		
Measuring spoons		

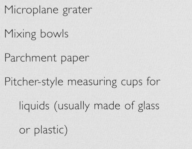
food processor

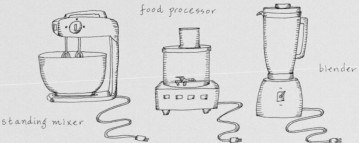
standing mixer
blender

"I learned how to measure with measuring cups.
I also learned that it is good to try foods you
don't know about because you might like them."

–*Robyn Kimmel, age 8*

Cooking Terms

Bake – to cook in an oven

Blend – to mix foods together until they are thoroughly incorporated—no lumps!

Boil – to cook a liquid until large bubbles form on the surface (water boils at 212 degrees F)

Broil – to cook food underneath a source of heat, such as the broiler in your oven

Chop – to use a chef's knife to cut ingredients into small pieces

Grate – to shred food with a box grater or with a grating blade on a food processor. When grating lemon or orange zest, it means using the smallest holes of a box grater or using a microplane grater

Grill – to cook over coals or wood in a grill; or to cook in a cast-iron or nonstick grill pan

Knead – to work dough with your hands in a folding-back and pressing-forward motion

Purée – to mix in a food processor or a blender until the food is very smooth, thick, and silky—like applesauce

Preheat – to get an oven hot before using it. This is important: Preheat your oven (according to the temperature given in the recipe) at least 15 minutes before using

Reduce – to let the water in a liquid evaporate so that the resulting liquid (broth, juice, etc.) is half its original volume and is thicker and more intensely flavored. This is done by bringing the liquid to a boil in a saucepan, lowering the heat, and letting it simmer until it reaches the desired quantity (i.e. 1 cup of liquid gets reduced to ½ cup)

Sauté – to cook food in a little bit of fat (oil, butter, etc.) in a pan over high heat on the stovetop

Simmer – to cook over low heat but maintaining little bubbles

Steam – to put food in a steamer basket over boiling water so that the steam "cooks" the food

Whip – to beat with an electric mixer or wire whisk until the ingredient (such as cream or eggs) thickens and increases in volume

Zest – this is the outermost colored skin of an orange, lemon, or lime. You can get long strips of zest using a vegetable peeler, or you can grate the zest on the fine holes of a box grater or microplane grater. You want to be careful not to include the white pith of the skin, which is bitter

Hot Chocolate
from Paris

This recipe comes directly from my friend Dorie Greenspan, who lives in Paris for part of the year. It is especially wonderful on cold winter mornings when you're still in your pj's.

7 ounces best-quality semi-sweet chocolate

3 cups whole milk

5 tablespoons sugar

1. Chop the chocolate into small pieces and set aside.

2. In a large saucepan, put the milk, sugar, and ⅓ cup of water. Cook over medium heat until it begins to boil. Remove from the heat and, using a wire whisk, whisk in the chopped chocolate. Whisk briskly until thick and smooth.

You can serve as is, or whip up, as follows:

3. If you have a handheld or immersion blender, use it to whip the hot chocolate for 30 seconds in the saucepan. Or carefully transfer the mixture to a blender and whip on high speed for 30 seconds. But first you must do two things: Put the top on the blender a bit askew so that hot air can escape, and cover the top with a thick towel so you don't burn your hand. **This must be done with an adult.**

Serve while it's very hot and frothy.

Serves 4

Wonderful on cold winter mornings
when you're still in your pjs.

Tomato Sunshine

Everyone will wonder what's in this delicious drink. Mix it up for your parents and ask them to guess! Tell them it's good for them, too.

1 cup V-8 juice
1 cup orange juice
2 teaspoons honey

1. Put all the ingredients in a large jar. Stir well or shake briskly.

2. Cover and chill in the refrigerator until very cold or serve immediately over ice.

Serves 2

Magic "Coffee"

This looks just like coffee and has a lovely sweet taste, but it uses no coffee and has no caffeine. It's pure black magic. I originally created this recipe with pickling spice, but I decided to use Danielle's suggestion instead!

3 tablespoons molasses
1 cinnamon stick
4 long strips of orange zest

1. Place 3 cups of cool water in a medium saucepan. Add the molasses, cinnamon stick, and orange zest. Bring to a boil. Lower the heat to a simmer and cook for 5 minutes, stirring occasionally. Pour the liquid through a mesh strainer into 4 warm coffee cups. Garnish each with a strip of the orange zest.

The mixture can be reheated.

Serves 4 (makes about 3 cups)

"I re-made the magic 'coffee' and substituted pickling spice (which burned my throat) with a cinnamon stick. Now I love it!"

~Danielle Hartog, age 11

Banana Frullato

A frullato is a fresh fruit milkshake, and it's a bright way to start any day.

1 large ripe banana
1 cup orange juice or pineapple juice
3 tablespoons sweetened condensed milk

1. Peel the banana and cut it into ½-inch-thick slices.
2. Put the banana slices in a blender with the juice, sweetened condensed milk, and 6 ice cubes.
3. Blend on high speed until very smooth and thick.

Serve over more ice.

Serves 2

Scrambled Eggs *au Fromage*

Bonjour! Fromage *means cheese in French. These luscious eggs have Gruyère cheese scrambled right into them. You can substitute Swiss cheese, but it won't have as much flavor. Serve with slices of* baguette *(crusty French bread) and finish with a cup of Hot Chocolate from Paris (see page 22). Bon appétit.*

4 extra-large eggs
2 ounces Gruyère cheese, in one piece
1 tablespoon unsalted butter

1. Break the eggs into a medium-size bowl.

2. Using a wire whisk or a hand-held mixer, beat the eggs until thoroughly mixed and frothy.

3. Add a large pinch of salt and freshly ground black pepper.

4. Grate the cheese on the large holes of a box grater (be careful not to grate your finger!).

5. Add all but a ½ cup of cheese to the eggs and mix briefly.

6. Melt the butter over medium heat in a small (I use an 8-inch) nonstick skillet. As soon as it melts (do not let it get brown), add the egg mixture.

7. Cook over medium heat, stirring constantly with a wooden spoon, until thick and creamy, about 5 minutes.

8. Divide the eggs onto 2 warm plates and sprinkle with the remaining cheese.

9. Serve immediately.

Serves 2

A Nice Omelette Crepe

Not quite an omelette (omelettes are thick) and not quite a crepe (crepes are thin and made with flour), this is what I call an omelette crepe: an ultra-thin, tender egg preparation that gets folded in thirds and hangs over your plate. If you don't like goat cheese (but do give it a try), you can omit the cheese and place a wide ribbon of strawberry preserves or Nutella (chocolate–hazelnut spread) down the center of the omelette crepe before it gets folded.

5 extra-large eggs
4 ounces fresh goat cheese, at room temperature
1½ tablespoons unsalted butter

1. Preheat the oven to 275 degrees.

2. Break the eggs into the bowl of an electric mixer, or use a regular bowl and a hand-held mixer. Crumble half of the goat cheese into the bowl. Add a large pinch of salt and freshly ground black pepper. Beat until smooth.

3. Melt ¾ tablespoon of the butter in a large nonstick sauté pan (I use a 12-inch pan). Add half of the egg mixture, making sure that it covers the bottom of the pan in a very thin layer. Cook over medium heat until the eggs begin to set but are still a little runny on top. Crumble half of the remaining cheese in a line down the center of the eggs.

4. While they are still soft, slip a spatula under one side of the eggs and fold them over the cheese. Then fold the other side over. You will have a very long log-shaped omelette crepe about 3 inches wide. Cook for 1½ minutes and carefully turn the crepe over. Cook for 1 minute longer and slip onto an oven-proof plate. Put the plate in the oven to keep warm.

5. Melt the remaining butter in the pan and repeat the process with the remaining egg mixture and cheese. Serve hot.

Serves 2

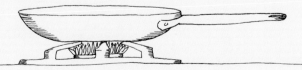

Smiley Eggs

Depending on the way you "paint" your eggs, the face will look like a smiley face or the man in the moon. The "paint" is pesto—a condiment made from fragrant basil, Parmesan cheese, and pignoli (pine) nuts. It tastes great and can be found in most supermarkets.

2 extra-large eggs
1 teaspoon unsalted butter
2 tablespoons prepared pesto

1. In a medium bowl, beat the eggs with 1 tablespoon water and a large pinch of salt until thoroughly mixed. If you don't mix it enough, you will have little white streaks through your egg face.

2. Melt the butter in a small nonstick frying pan (I use a 7-inch pan).

3. Pour in the beaten eggs. Let the eggs cook over low heat until they begin to set, about 2 minutes.

4. Using a small spoon, make a smiling face: Put 1 teaspoon of pesto where each eye should be and make a smile using the remaining pesto.

5. Cover the pan. Cook for 1 to 2 minutes longer until the eggs are just firm. Do not overcook. The eggs will get a little puffy and add great interest to the face.

6. Place the pan on a large heat-proof plate. Smile and eat from the pan.

Serves 1

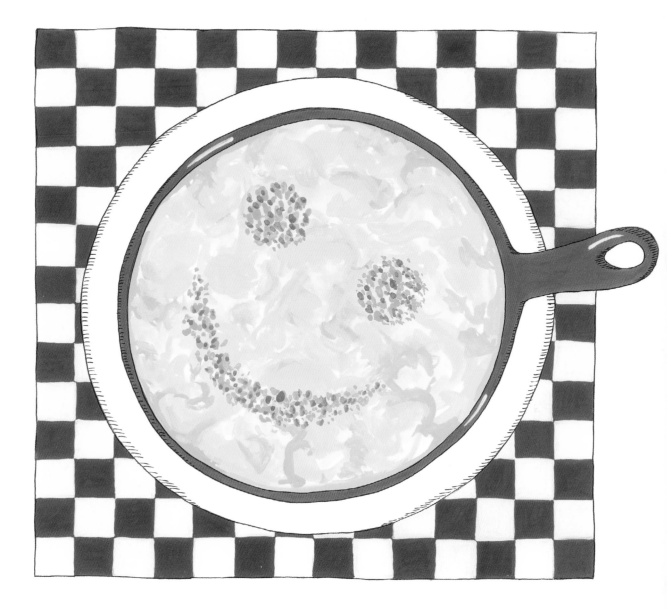

Smile and eat from the pan!

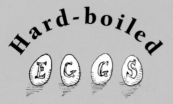

Hard-boiled EGGS

6 fresh extra-large eggs

1. Put the eggs in a small, stainless-steel or enamel saucepan. Cover them with cold water.

2. Bring the water to a boil over high heat. When the water is bubbling, and the bubbles are big, turn the heat to low. Cook the eggs, uncovered at a simmer, for about 14 minutes.

3. Remove the saucepan from the heat and put it into the sink. Carefully pour off the water, then run cold water over the eggs until they cool.

4. Refrigerate the eggs until very cold, about 2 hours. (Or immediately make a Birthday "Egg Cake" with one or more while they are slightly warm (see page 31).

5. When the eggs are cold, roll them on the counter while you gently press on them so that the shells break up a bit. Peel them carefully, making sure to remove all the little bits of shell. Otherwise, they will c-r-r-unch in your mouth.

Makes 6

Hard-boiled Eggs
and Fun Things to Do with Them

There are countless things you can do with a hard-boiled egg, that is, once you've learned how to make it. You can eat it out of hand; you can slice it, mash it, stuff it. The egg is full of great nutrition—vitamins and minerals—and it comes apart, too. You can eat the jiggly but firm white part first, and then the yellow ball, also known as the yolk. A hard-boiled egg costs about 12 cents. It's a bargain.

Eggs come in different sizes: Your supermarket probably has them in large, extra large, and jumbo. I use extra large because my mother always did. White eggs come from hens with white feathers and white ear lobes. Brown eggs come from hens with red feathers and red ear lobes. There is no difference in taste or nutrition between white and brown eggs.

Eggs must be fresh, so check the date on the egg carton. If you don't know whether an egg is fresh, put it in a bowl of cold water. If it floats to the top, don't use it! And never use an egg that has any cracks. Making a hard-boiled egg is simple if you follow a few rules.

Black-and-White Sesame Eggs

Hard–boiled eggs are halved and coated with tasty, crunchy seeds that make them look like little buried treasures.

3 tablespoons white sesame seeds
I tablespoon black sesame seeds
2 hard-boiled eggs, chilled

1. Put the white sesame seeds in a small non-stick skillet. Place the skillet over medium heat and toast the sesame seeds until golden, about I minute. Shake the skillet back and forth to prevent sticking.

2. Remove the skillet from the heat and let cool.

3. Stir in the black sesame seeds and ½ teaspoon of salt.

4. Cut the eggs in half lengthwise and dip the cut halves into the sesame mixture.

Serves 2

Birthday "Egg Cake"

Insert a candle and make a wish.

I thick slice of challah or brioche
I½ tablespoons light mayonnaise
I warm hard-boiled egg, thinly sliced

1. Trim the challah or brioche with a small, sharp knife or a cookie cutter to make a circular shape that is 3½ inches in diameter. Lightly toast the bread.

2. Layer the egg slices on the toast so that they slightly overlap but lie as flat as possible.

3. Using a butter knife, spread the mayonnaise over the egg slices, adding a little on the sides, as though you were icing a birthday cake.

4. Sprinkle with salt. Eat immediately.

Serves I

Marble Eggs

This is an adaptation of a Chinese recipe. After steeping in black tea for two hours, the eggs get a network of tiny, intricate lines that resemble marble. Star anise tastes like licorice but is shaped like a star, and you can find it in Asian food stores and many supermarkets. Serve with freshly cut oranges (for good luck, say the Chinese) and a stack of puffy rice cakes.

6 hard-boiled eggs
2 tablespoons loose black tea leaves
2 star anise, broken into pieces

1. Tap each egg lightly on the counter to make small cracks all over the shell.

2. Place the eggs in a medium saucepan. Add the tea, star anise, and ½ tablespoon salt. Cover with cold water. Bring to a boil.

3. Reduce the heat to very low and cook, with the lid askew, for 2 hours.

4. Add more water if necessary to keep the eggs covered. Let the eggs cool in the liquid.

5. Remove the eggs and peel (discard the liquid). Serve chilled.

You can store the eggs for up to 3 days.
Makes 6

Real maple syrup is made
from the sap of maple trees.

Puffy Maple Pancake

This is perfect for a weekend brunch. You will be amazed at how this maple cloud puffs up and holds its shape. The instructions say to separate the egg whites from the egg yolks. You do this by carefully cracking each egg on the side of a bowl and letting only the clear liquid dribble into a bowl. Carefully place the yolk in another bowl. Use real maple syrup (not pancake syrup). Real maple syrup is made from the sap of maple trees.

4 extra-large eggs
6 tablespoons real maple syrup
1 tablespoon unsalted butter

1. Preheat the oven to 400 degrees.

2. Separate the egg whites from the eggs yolks as described above. In the bowl of an electric mixer (or using a bowl and a hand-held mixer), beat together the yolks, 2 tablespoons maple syrup, and freshly ground black pepper for several minutes until thick.

3. Put the egg whites into another large bowl and, using clean beaters or a whisk, beat the whites with ¼ teaspoon salt until they look like thick whipped cream with firm peaks. This will take several minutes. Spoon the whites into the yolks. Using a flexible rubber spatula, gently mix together until completely incorporated.

4. Melt the butter in a large ovenproof nonstick skillet (I use a 10-inch skillet) over medium heat. Add the egg mixture to the pan and lower the heat. Cook for 2 minutes, until the eggs are just set. Shake the pan to check; it should jiggle only a little.

5. Place the skillet in the hot oven. Cook for 5 to 6 minutes, until puffy and golden. Do not overcook or the pancake will collapse and be dry. Drizzle with the remaining syrup. Serve immediately.

Serves 2

DINER

Cheddar–Pepper Grits

This is "comfort food" at its best, served soft and runny or chilled and baked in squares. Hominy grits are made from white corn that is coarsely milled and cured with lye to soften the kernels. Quick-cooking cornmeal, or polenta, can be substituted.

1 cup quick-cooking grits

1½ cups shredded sharp yellow cheddar

1 tablespoon unsalted butter

1. Put 4 cups of water plus 1 teaspoon salt in a medium saucepan. Bring to a rapid boil. Lower heat to medium-high and, using a small wire whisk, slowly add the grits, whisking constantly until smooth. Cook for 5 minutes, stirring frequently with the whisk, until thick.

2. Add 1 cup of the cheese, butter, and lots of freshly ground black pepper. Stir until smooth and cook 2 minutes longer, stirring, until very thick.

3. Serve immediately with the remaining cheese scattered on top. Or, if desired, spray an 8 × 8-inch glass baking dish with cooking spray. Pour grits into dish and top with the remaining cheese. Bake at 350 degrees for 12 minutes.

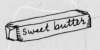

Serves 8

FOOD

Lemony Potato Hash

Use thin-skinned little red potatoes, also known as new potatoes, for this unusual breakfast side dish. Crispy and sun-kissed with a splash of lemon.

1 pound red new potatoes
2 tablespoons olive oil
1 lemon

1. Wash the potatoes and dry well with paper towels. Cut the potatoes, with skin on, into ¼ inch cubes.

2. Heat the oil in a 12-inch nonstick skillet. Add the potatoes. Cook over high heat, stirring often, so that the potatoes do not stick. Cook until the potatoes turn golden brown.

3. After 10 minutes, add ½ teaspoon salt and freshly ground black pepper.

4. Continue to cook until the potatoes are tender and crispy, about 6 minutes.

5. Grate the zest of the lemon and scatter over the potatoes.

6. Cut the lemon in half and squeeze 1 teaspoon of juice over the potatoes. Cook for 1 minute longer. Serve immediately.

Serves 4

1.

2.

3.

Silver-Dollar Sausage Patties

It is great fun to make your own sausage and you can do it in five minutes. Because you use ground turkey instead of pork, these are so much better (and healthier) than anything you can find in the supermarket.

12 ounces ground turkey

3 small garlic cloves

2 teaspoons ground cumin

1. Place the turkey in a medium bowl.

2. Peel the garlic cloves and press them (one at a time) through a garlic press.

3. Add the pressed garlic to the turkey.

4. Add the cumin, ½ teaspoon salt, and ¼ teaspoon black pepper.

5. Using a fork, mash the ingredients to mix them well.

6. Cover and refrigerate for 1 hour to let the flavors mingle. Or you can cook it immediately, if you're very hungry.

7. Wash your hands well. Using your hands, form the mixture into 12 flat patties, each about 2 inches in diameter and ¼ inch thick. Wash your hands well again.

8. Place a large nonstick skillet over medium-high heat until hot. Add the sausage patties and cook them on one side until browned, about 2 minutes.

9. Carefully turn the patties over and cook them on the other side until browned and cooked through, about 2 minutes longer. Serve immediately.

Makes 12

Bacon "Candy"

Doesn't this sound delicious? It's great with French toast, pancakes, or any kind of egg dish. The special flavor comes from five-spice powder, which is a Chinese seasoning made from cinnamon, cloves, coriander, ginger, and black pepper. If you can't find it easily, try using pumpkin pie spice. Confectioners' sugar is also known as powdered sugar or icing sugar and it looks like cornstarch or baby powder. Be sure to read the label before you cook with it!

8 thick slices of bacon, about ½ pound
1 tablespoon five-spice powder
2 tablespoons confectioners' sugar

1. Preheat the oven to 375 degrees.

2. Carefully separate the slices of bacon.

3. In a small bowl, mix the five-spice powder and confectioners' sugar. Sprinkle each slice of bacon with the mixture to coat evenly.

4. Place the bacon slices several inches apart on a rimmed baking sheet.

5. Bake for 15 minutes, then carefully pour off the fat **(do this with an adult)**.

6. Bake for 10 minutes longer, or until crisp. Remove from the oven and let sit for 1 to 2 minutes before serving.

Makes 8 slices

Warm, comforting and delicious.
Make them for a friend!

Warm Buttermilk Biscuits

These flaky biscuits are sooo delicious when spread with sweet butter and topped with strawberry-orange marmalade or grape jelly that you make yourself (see page 45). Have fun rolling the dough with a rolling pin and cutting out the biscuits with a cookie cutter.

2¾ cups self-rising flour, plus more for kneading
8 tablespoons unsalted butter, at room temperature
1 cup buttermilk, at room temperature

1. Preheat the oven to 400 degrees.

2. Place the flour in the bowl of a food processor. Cut the butter into small pieces and put one teaspoon aside for later. Put the rest of the butter into the food processor with the flour. Pulse the food processor 20 times; this means to turn it on and off very quickly to mix the butter into the flour. The flour will look crumbly.

3. Pour the flour into a bowl. And the buttermilk and, using a wooden spoon, stir until the buttermilk is absorbed and the flour starts to pull away from the side of the bowl. This will only take a few minutes—you don't want to overdo it or the biscuits will be tough.

4. Sprinkle more flour onto a large board or onto the countertop. Put the ball of dough on the board and knead it with your hands: that means to press the dough down firmly and fold it over several times until the dough pretty much sticks together. It may look a bit lumpy, but that's okay.

5. Pat a little flour onto a rolling pin. Roll out the dough to a thickness of ½ inch. Cut out circles with a 2-inch round cookie cutter. Using a paper towel, spread the remaining teaspoon of butter on a rimmed baking sheet. Place the biscuits on the baking sheet and bake for 18 to 20 minutes, or until the tops are golden. You may put them under the broiler for 10 seconds if you want them more golden.

Makes 14

1.

2.

3.

Petits Pains
au Chocolat

These small, elegant pastries are incredibly easy to prepare and will make you feel like a professional chef! Filled with oozing chocolate, they are delicious with a cold glass of milk or doubly delicious with a cup of Hot Chocolate from Paris (see page 22)!

I sheet frozen puff pastry, about 8 ounces
4 ounces thin semi-sweet chocolate bar
I extra-large egg

1. Preheat the oven to 400 degrees.

2. Thaw the pastry at room temperature for about 20 minutes, until it is bendable but still very cold. Cut the pastry sheet into 12 squares.

3. Break or cut the chocolate into 12 small rectangular pieces, about 2 inches long by ¾ inch wide. Place the chocolate on one edge of the pastry and roll tight, finishing with the seam on the bottom.

4. Line a baking sheet with parchment paper. Place the rolled-up pastries, seam side down on the parchment. Press the open edges of the pastry with the tines of a fork to seal.

5. Separate the egg. In a small bowl, whisk together the egg yolk and I tablespoon of water. This is known as an "egg wash." Using a pastry brush, brush the tops of the pastry with egg wash. Bake for 20 minutes, or until puffed and golden brown.

6. Let cool.

Makes 12

Toasty Oats with Cider Syrup

*I never cared much for hot cereal when I was young, but no
one ever made it for me this way. Here, old-fashioned oats
are drizzled with hot cider syrup and topped with a billow of
whipped cream.*

4 cups real apple cider, refrigerated
2 cups old-fashioned rolled oats
½ cup heavy cream

1. Put 2 cups of apple cider in a small saucepan. Bring to a
   boil, lower the heat to medium, and cook until the cider is
   reduced to ½ cup, about 25 minutes. Set aside. This can be
   made one day ahead and reheated gently.

2. To make the oatmeal: In a medium saucepan, put the
   remaining 2 cups of apple cider, 1½ cups of water, and
   ¼ teaspoon salt. Bring to a boil. Lower the heat to medium
   and add the oatmeal. Cook over medium heat for 5
   minutes, stirring frequently. Add 2 tablespoons of the heavy
   cream. Cook for 1 or 2 minutes longer, until the oatmeal is
   the desired thickness.

3. Meanwhile, whip the remaining cream using a wire
   whisk or electric beaters. Whip just until soft
   peaks form. Divide the oatmeal
   among four bowls. Top with
   whipped cream and drizzle
   with warm cider syrup.
   Serve immediately.

Serves 4

Great 1-2-3 Idea

To Make Cinnamon-Sugar:

In a small bowl, stir together 1 cup sugar and 1½ tablespoons ground cinnamon. Pour or spoon the mixture into a jar.
Lasts indefinitely.

Makes 1 cup

Dutch Breakfast

In Holland, they serve this treat for breakfast! But it's a great snack any time.

1 slice of white bread
1 teaspoon unsalted butter, at room temperature
2 tablespoons chocolate sprinkles

1. Spread the butter on the bread with a butter knife and scatter sprinkles over the bread.

Serves 1

Sweet Almond Toast

This is best made with challah, a braided egg bread you can buy in many bakeries and supermarkets. You also can use brioche or thick slices of good white bread.

4 ¾-inch thick slices of challah
4 tablespoons sweetened condensed milk
½ cup sliced almonds, with skins

1. Preheat the oven to 375 degrees.
2. Place the bread on a baking sheet.
3. Spread 1 tablespoon of the sweetened condensed milk evenly over the surface of each slice of bread.
4. Sprinkle each slice of bread with the almonds, about 2 tablespoons, to cover completely.
5. Bake for 15 to 18 minutes, until almonds are golden and the condensed milk has turned golden brown.
6. Let cool for several minutes, but serve warm.

Makes 4

Creamy Homemade Butter

This is the very best butter—now say that three times quickly!—and so easy to make at home. And all you need is one ingredient: heavy cream. You beat it and beat it and beat it and after a while the solids separate from the whey (the milky liquid), leaving you with a ball of pale yellow . . . wow . . . butter! You can make honey butter and strawberry butter, too. Or add freshly snipped chives and lime zest for a savory butter that you can spread on corn. This recipe makes 1/2 cup of butter, which is the same as one stick of store-bought butter.

1 cup heavy cream, chilled

1. Put the cream in the bowl of an electric mixer (or use a regular bowl and a hand-held mixer). Beat on high for 7 minutes. The cream will begin to thicken and become smooth. Then it will change suddenly and it will separate into small solids and a milky liquid (this is buttermilk). It will slosh around for a bit and then a few seconds later, a ball of butter will form that is separate from the milky liquid.

2. Drain off the buttermilk (you can drink it or save it for another use) and press down on the butter to release all the liquid.

3. Add a pinch of salt and stir well.

4. Put the butter in a dish. You can spread it on bread right now!

5. Or cover and refrigerate; the flavor will develop. Fresh butter will last up to 1 week.

Makes ½ cup

Flavored Butters

To make the flavored butters below, stir the flavoring ingredients into the butter before you refrigerate.

Honey Butter	Strawberry Butter	Chive Butter
2 tablespoons honey	**3 tablespoons of strawberry jam**	**4 teaspoons finely chopped chives**
¼ teaspoon ground nutmeg	**¼ teaspoon ground cinnamon**	**½ teaspoon grated lime or lemon zest**

Extra-Special Cream Cheeses

These flavored cream cheeses are great to spread on toasted bagels,
English muffins, corn muffins, or pumpernickel bread.

Chocolate

8 ounces cream cheese, softened

⅓ cup Nutella
(chocolate-hazelnut spread)

1 tablespoons confectioners' sugar

1. Put the ingredients in a medium-sized bowl.
2. Using a hand-held mixer, mix until the ingredients are well blended. Do not overmix.
3. Cover and chill.

Makes 1 heaping cup

Maple–Raisin

8 ounces cream cheese, softened

3 tablespoons real maple syrup

heaping ⅓ cup raisins

1. Place all ingredients in bowl of food processor.
2. Process briefly until all ingredients are incorporated.
3. Do not overprocess.
4. Cover and chill.

Makes about 1¼ cups

Honey–Walnut

8 ounces cream cheese, softened

½ cup coarsely chopped walnuts

3 tablespoons honey

1. Put the walnuts in a small nonstick skillet.
2. Heat for 1 to 2 minutes over medium heat, stirring often, until the nuts are toasted. Let cool.
3. Place the cream cheese and honey in a medium-sized bowl.
4. Using a hand-held mixer, beat just until smooth.
5. Stir in the nuts. Cover and chill.

Makes 1¼ cups

Strawberry "Cheesecake"

8 ounces cream cheese, softened

3 tablespoons strawberry preserves

¼ cup confectioners' sugar

1. Put the ingredients in a medium-sized bowl.
2. Using a hand-held mixer, beat just until smooth.
3. Cover and chill.

Makes 1 heaping cup

Quick Strawberry–Orange Marmalade

Marmalade can be complicated to make and can take hours to cook. But this version is as easy and quick as can be.

1 pound small ripe strawberries

¼ cup sugar

12 ounces good-quality orange marmalade

1. Wash and dry the berries. Remove stems.

2. Cut the berries in half and place in a non-reactive (not aluminum) medium saucepan.

3. Stir in the sugar. Let sit for 15 minutes.

4. Cook the strawberries over high heat for 2 minutes, stirring constantly.

5. Add the marmalade and, stirring carefully because it is very hot, cook on high heat until the marmalade is melted.

6. Bring the mixture to a boil. Boil for 5 minutes, stirring once or twice.

7. Lower the heat to medium and cook for 15 minutes, stirring often. At this point the mixture will be bubbling away.

8. When the mixture is thick and coats the back of a wooden spoon, remove it from the heat and let it cool.

9. Transfer to a pretty bowl or jar. Cover and refrigerate until ready to use.

Makes about 2 cups

The Grapiest Grape Jelly

This is the wobbliest, grapiest, most delicious jelly you'll ever eat!

2 cups purple grape juice

2 tablespoons honey

1 packet unflavored gelatin

1. Put the juice in a medium saucepan.

2. Stir in the honey and bring to a boil.

3. Lower the heat to medium and sprinkle the gelatin powder over the juice. Using a small wire whisk, stir the gelatin into the juice until it dissolves. Make sure there are no lumps.

4. Continue to cook and whisk for 3 minutes.

5. Remove from the heat and pour the juice into a 8 x 8-inch square glass pan. Let cool.

6. Refrigerate for 3 hours, or until very firm.

7. Scrape up the jelly with a spoon and put into a jar. Keep refrigerated.

Makes about 1¾ cups

What to Have for Lunch

Great 1-2-3 Idea

Two Neat Things to Do with Chicken Wings

1. Put the cooked wings on a rack on a rimmed baking sheet. Preheat the broiler. Broil the wings for 5 minutes. Sprinkle with salt and pepper.

2. Remove the meat from the cooked chicken wings and add to the soup or to a pasta dish.

Cure-a-Cold Chicken Soup

This recipe is sooo simple and good, your mom might ask you for the recipe.

2 pounds chicken wings
4 scallions
2-inch piece of fresh ginger

1. Remove the wing tips with a small knife and discard. Put the wings in an 8-quart pot with a cover. Add 12 cups of cold water and 1 tablespoon of salt.

2. Thinly slice 3 of the scallions (white and green parts) and add to the pot. Peel the ginger with a small knife or scrape away the peel with the edge of a spoon, and slice into thin rounds. Add to the pot.

3. Bring to a full boil. Lower the heat and cover the pot. Cook over low heat for 45 minutes; the broth should be simmering.

4. Remove the chicken wings with tongs and put them on a platter. **With the help of an adult**, strain the soup through a fine-mesh sieve set over a clean pot. Bring to a boil, lower the heat to medium, and cook for 20 minutes or until the stock is reduced to 10 cups. If using later, chill the stock, skim the fat, and reheat. Serve hot with the remaining scallions thinly sliced in soup bowls or mugs.

Serves 8

Homemade Soup— Good for when
you're on top of the world,
or feeling under the weather.

Great 1-2-3 Idea

Fun Add-ons for Your Soup

1. Spice it up with hot sauce

2. Sprinkle with freshly grated Parmesan cheese

3. Top with finely chopped chives

Steamy Creamy Tomato Soup

This is fresher tasting and more delicious than tomato soup that comes from a can. For fun, you can whip a little additional heavy cream until thick, plop it on top of the soup, and watch it melt away. Very good with Warm Buttermilk Biscuits (see page 39).

⅔ cup tomato sauce
2 tablespoons heavy cream
2 teaspoons honey

1. Put all ingredients plus ⅓ cup water in a small saucepan. Add salt and freshly ground black pepper to taste. Bring just to a boil, stirring constantly with a wooden spoon.

2. When nice and hot, pour into a mug. Let cool a bit and drink away.

Note: You may also use a spoon.

Serves 1

100 Carrot–Ginger Soup

This soup is made with 100 baby carrots or 10 large carrots. Naturally sweet and velvety, the soup's special taste comes from fresh ginger juice that you squeeze yourself.

100 baby carrots or 10 large carrots (1½ pounds)
4-inch piece of fresh ginger
½ cup heavy cream

1. If using whole carrots, trim and peel them and cut them into 1-inch pieces. Put the carrot pieces or baby carrots in a 4-quart saucepan with 4 cups water and 1½ teaspoons salt. Bring to a boil, lower the heat, and cover the pot. Cook for 30 minutes, or until the carrots are very soft.

2. With a slotted spoon, transfer the carrots to the bowl of a food processor. Begin to process, slowly adding the cooking water as you go. All the water should be added.

3. Peel the ginger with a small knife or scrape the peel away with the edge of a spoon. Grate the ginger on the large holes of a box grater. Put the grated ginger in the center of a paper towel. Gather the corners to make a little pouch. Squeeze the ginger over a small bowl to extract the ginger juice. You will have about 1 tablespoon.

4. Add the ginger juice to the processor with 6 tablespoons of the cream. Process briefly, adding salt and pepper to taste.

5. Transfer to a saucepan and heat until hot. Pour into soup bowls and drizzle with the remaining cream.

Serves 5 to 6

10 Things to Do with Chicken Salad

1. Stuff it into a scooped-out tomato

2. Mound it on top of a halved avocado

3. Make an open-face sandwich

4. Fill a toasted pita pocket

5. Add diced mango and toasted almonds

6. Add chopped apples and curry powder

7. Add fresh tarragon and minced red onion

8. Add diced red bell peppers and chopped scallions

9. Add peas and crumbled bacon

10. Put on top of a toasted English muffin; cover with cheese and broil until bubbly

Chicken Salad 1-2-3

How to Make It! What to Do with It!

This ancient Chinese method of cooking a whole chicken was meant to save fuel. A pot of cold water, with a chicken in it, is brought to a boil, and then the heat is turned off. The pot stays covered (no peeking!) until the chicken is cooked, about three hours. You need to *listen* carefully for the water to boil; it should take 20 to 25 minutes. The pot's cover will start to shake a bit and you'll hear a thump-thump—that's the water boiling. A bonus: The resulting chicken broth can be used in other recipes! Cook it until it is reduced by half.

Chicken Salad

4-pound chicken
½ cup mayonnaise
I cup finely chopped celery

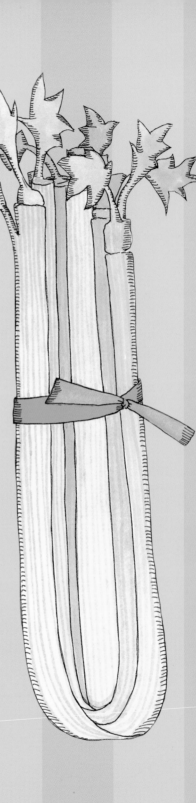

1. Wash the chicken thoroughly. Discard the giblets from the cavity (the chicken liver, neck, and heart). Using a piece of kitchen string, tie the ends of the legs together.

2. Put the chicken in an 8-quart pot with a cover. Cover with cold water, about 5 quarts (20 cups). Add 2 tablespoons kosher salt and I tablespoon whole black peppercorns. Cover the pot. Cook over high heat for 20 to 25 minutes, until you can hear the water in the pot boiling rapidly. **Do not lift the cover.**

3. Turn off the heat. Let sit for 3 hours. No peeking!

4. Remove the chicken from the broth. Put the chicken on a platter to cool.

5. Remove the skin and bones and cut the chicken into small pieces. Be sure to remove the meat from the wings. Put chicken in a bowl. Discard the skin and bones.

6. In a bowl, combine the chicken with the mayonnaise and celery. Add salt and freshly ground black pepper to taste. Cover and refrigerate until ready to use.

Serves 6

1-2-3
Peanut Butter

Peanut butter is the glue that holds so many great sandwiches together. Accompany any of the sandwiches on the next page with a cold glass of milk.

If you or the people you are making sandwiches for are allergic to peanuts, but not to other nuts, you may substitute almond butter or hazelnut butter and still be very happy. Or turn to another page for more non-nutty lunch and snack ideas!

Make Your Own Peanut Butter

The best food is the food you make yourself. Homemade peanut butter is clean and fresh tasting and you can control how smooth or chunky it is. Simply remove the reddish husks from store-bought peanuts and whirl them away in your blender.

2 cups unsalted roasted peanuts
3 tablespoons vegetable oil
½ tablespoon honey

1. Remove the reddish husks from the peanuts.

2. Put 1 cup of the peanuts, 1½ tablespoons of the vegetable oil, the honey and ½ teaspoon salt in a food processor.

3. Process until the peanut butter is rather smooth.

4. Add the remaining peanuts and oil and process again until it reaches the desired consistency. This will take about 2 minutes. (It will always look a little chunky and not like the smooth stuff you get in the supermarket.)

5. Transfer to a jar, cover, and refrigerate. Keeps up to 1 week.

Makes 1 cup

PB&J . . .
Themes *and* Variations

The Classic
White bread, peanut butter, jelly

Try The Grapiest Grape Jelly on page 45,
or another favorite

Health Nut
Wheat bread, peanut butter,
apple butter

Cowboy
Flour tortillas, peanut butter,
crispy bacon (crisped in a pan)

Black Forest
Pumpernickel bagel, peanut butter,
sun-dried cherries

Bananadana
Cinnamon-raisin bread,
peanut butter, sliced bananas

Sweetie
Challah toast, peanut butter,
chocolate sprinkles

Country
Toasted corn muffin,
peanut butter, strawberry jam

Splendido
Italian bread, peanut butter,
white chocolate shavings

Frenchie
Croissant, peanut butter,
melted chocolate

Dreamy
Date-nut bread,
peanut butter, honey

Belgian
White bread, peanut butter,
Nutella (chocolate-hazelnut spread)

Today's Special
Pound cake, peanut butter,
mini-marshmallows
Under the broiler

A Can of Tuna Fish . . .

1.
My Favorite Tuna Salad

6-ounce can white tuna packed in oil
2½ tablespoons mayonnaise
2 tablespoons pickle relish

1. Drain the tuna and put in a bowl.
2. Mix in the mayonnaise until mushy.
3. Add the relish and stir well.
4. Add a pinch of salt and pepper and stir again.

Makes enough for 2 sandwiches

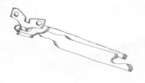

2.
Bagel Tuna Melt

6 ounce can white tuna packed in water
I large bagel (sesame is my favorite)
I cup shredded very sharp yellow cheddar

1. Preheat the oven to 400 degrees.
2. Drain the tuna and put in a bowl with the cheese. Using a fork, mash them together well.
3. Carefully slice the bagel in half—or get an adult to help—and toast both pieces on a baking sheet in the oven.
4. Add black pepper to the tuna to taste.
5. Pile the tuna and cheese mixture on the toasted bagel halves.
6. Place on the baking sheet.
7. Bake for 8 minutes. Put under the broiler for I minute or until bubbly.

Serves 2

Four Things to Do with It

3.

Tuna–Olive Spread

Great for spreading on crackers or on thin white bread for tea sandwiches.

3 ounces cream cheese

6-ounce can white tuna packed in oil

⅓ cup pimiento-stuffed olives, juice reserved

1. Put the cream cheese in a shallow bowl and let come to room temperature.

2. Drain most of the oil from the can of tuna, and add the tuna to the cream cheese. Mash well together using a fork.

3. Rinse the olives in a small strainer. Pat dry. Finely chop the olives and add to the tuna mixture. Add a little of the olive juice and salt and pepper to taste.

Makes 1⅓ cups

4.

The Can Itself!

Using a can opener, remove the top and bottom lids of an imported 6-ounce tuna fish can (or any can with two removable lids). You will have a 4-inch ring.

Be very careful of the sharp edges!

This makes a great mold for:

1. frying a perfect egg

2. forming mashed potatoes

3. as a big cookie cutter for shortcakes or scones

Clean it really well first!

"The tuna-olive spread was very good. I loved that. We put it in a nice little bowl and served it as a snack. Mom used it as an hors d'oeuvre before dinner."

–Julia Miller, age 11

Mac-and-Cheese

Once upon a time, I had so many slices of American cheese in my fridge, I didn't know what to do. So . . . I invented this simple version of every-one's favorite recipe. You can use familiar elbow macaroni or the less familiar shape called campanelle ("little bells"). If you want this even cheesier, just melt a few more slices of cheese!

4 ounces elbow macaroni
4 ounces American cheese, about 7 slices
1 tablespoon unsalted butter

1. Bring a large saucepan of salted water to a boil. Add the pasta and cook for about 10 minutes, until just tender.

2. Meanwhile, put ¼ cup water and the cheese in a medium size saucepan. Bring just to a boil. Immediately lower the heat to medium and stir with a wooden spoon until the cheese melts, about 3 minutes. Add the butter and continue to stir for 1 minute, or until you have a smooth sauce.

3. Put a colander in the sink and, **with the help of an adult**, drain the pasta. Return the drained pasta to the large saucepan and pour the cheese sauce over the pasta.

4. Add salt and freshly ground black pepper to taste. Stir gently while reheating the pasta.

Serves 2 or 3

1-2-3 Tip

When draining pasta, you should have an adult with you. You can skim the pasta from the water with a slotted spoon and put it in a colander, or you can dump the contents of the pot directly into a colander set in the sink. You need to be careful as the steam is very hot.

Mac-and-cheese,
One of life's great comforts!

Crazy Leg Drumsticks

The nice herby taste comes from pesto—an uncooked Italian sauce made from fresh basil, garlic, and pignoli nuts. You can find it today in any supermarket. A dusting of Parmesan cheese turns into a crispy coating.

⅓ cup prepared pesto
4 large chicken legs
½ cup grated Parmesan cheese

1. Preheat the oven to 375 degrees.

2. Spread pesto all over each chicken leg to cover. Sprinkle cheese all over each leg, except for the bottom where it will sit on the baking sheet. (You don't want the cheese to burn.) Lightly press the cheese onto the chicken so it will stick. Sprinkle with freshly ground black pepper.

3. Lightly spray a rimmed baking sheet with cooking spray. Place the legs on the baking sheet.

4. Bake for 35 minutes, until chicken is crispy and golden.

Serves 4

Burger-on-a-Stick

In many Middle Eastern countries, ground beef or lamb is grilled on sticks or skewers. These are known as kebabs. Press the mixture with your hands onto 8-inch wooden skewers and broil them to your liking.

¾ pound ground beef chuck
I small garlic clove
½ teaspoon ground cumin

1. Turn the broiler on high.

2. Put the ground beef in a medium-sized bowl. Peel the garlic and push it through a garlic press. Add to the beef. Add the cumin, ½ teaspoon salt, and freshly ground black pepper and mix well.

3. Divide the mixture into 4 mounds. Using your hands, squeeze the mixture onto 4 wooden skewers, making a long cylinder that is about 6 inches long and 2 inches wide. Flatten the mixture slightly and put the skewers on a rimmed baking sheet. Cover the exposed wood of skewers with foil so the skewers don't burn.

4. Broil for 3 to 4 minutes, until just cooked through. Do not overcook. Serve immediately.

Note: If you don't want to broil the kebabs, you can bake them at 375 degrees for 8 minutes. (You don't need to cover exposed skewers with foil.)

Makes 4

Special Ingredient: Cumin

Cumin is a wonderful, earthy spice that is used in many cuisines, including Mexican, Middle Eastern, Indian, and Tex-Mex.

"I must say Burger-on-a-Stick was probably the best success we had. It would be great for a kid that comes home in a grumpy/hungry mood. In other words, it's quick and fast to cook."

–Nick Green, age 11

These wings fly right off the plate!

Sticky Finger Wings

You might not be able to guess what's in this Asian-tasting chicken but you will love it anyway. The shiny brown color and flavor comes from tamari (soy sauce made without wheat flour) and brown sugar. Sometimes chicken wings are packaged as "wingettes" and are already cut in two; in that case, you will need 12 pieces.

6 very large chicken wings
¼ cup tamari
¼ cup dark brown sugar

1. Preheat the oven to 350 degrees.

2. Each wing has three sections. Cut off and discard the smallest section (called the wing tip). Cut the remainder of each wing through the joint. Skip this step if you're using "wingettes."

3. Mix the tamari and sugar in a medium-sized bowl until the sugar dissolves. Add freshly ground black pepper. Add the chicken wings and mix. Marinate for 1 hour, turning the wings several times.

4. Using tongs, remove the wings from the marinade and place them on a rimmed baking sheet.

5. Bake for 15 minutes. Using tongs, carefully turn the wings over. Spoon or brush a little marinade over the wings.

6. Bake for 10 minutes longer. Turn again and brush with a little marinade. The wings should be dark brown and shiny. Bake for 5 minutes longer. Serve the wings on a platter and discard the marinade.

Serves 3 or 4

Crunchy Fried Tomatoes

*These are a crunchy, colorful accompaniment to sandwiches and salads.
Or you can eat a whole stack of them for lunch. They're also great on
top of a burger! They can be made with red, yellow, or green tomatoes
as long as they're firm.*

4 medium-size firm tomatoes (red, yellow, or green)
1 cup stone-ground yellow cornmeal
Vegetable oil for frying

1. Wash the tomatoes and dry well. Slice off the top and bottom
   ends. Cut each tomato horizontally into 3 thick slices.

2. Place the cornmeal on a flat plate. Dredge both sides of each
   tomato slice in cornmeal, pressing down lightly. Make sure the cut
   surfaces are thickly coated (sides will not get coated).

3. Heat ¼ inch of oil in a large skillet. When hot, carefully add the
   tomatoes in one layer—**you may want some adult assistance
   here.**

4. Cook over medium high heat for 2 minutes on each side, or until
   crispy and golden brown. Do not overcook, as you want the
   tomatoes to retain their shape. You may need to do this in 2
   batches, adding oil as needed.

5. Drain the tomatoes on paper towels. Sprinkle with salt and freshly
   ground black pepper. Serve 3 slices per person.

Serves 4

1.

2.

3.

In France, fries are called "frites"
In England, they're called "chips"

Parmesan Fries

These baked fries are every bit as tasty as fried fries. They are much healthier and easier to make, too. Use Idaho, or russet, potatoes for the best texture. Grapeseed oil helps the fries get really crispy, but you may use olive oil or vegetable oil, too.

3 large Idaho potatoes, about 1¾ pounds
4 tablespoons vegetable oil
⅓ cup freshly grated Parmesan cheese

1. Preheat the oven to 375 degrees.

2. Peel the potatoes. Wash them and pat dry with paper towels. Cut into fries about 3 inches long and ⅓ inch wide and deep. Use a crinkle cutter if possible. Place them in a large bowl and drizzle with 3 tablespoons of the oil. Stir until the potatoes are coated. Add ½ teaspoon salt and freshly ground black pepper and toss again.

3. Coat a rimmed baking sheet with the remaining 1 tablespoon of oil. Place the potatoes in a single layer on the baking sheet. Bake for 20 minutes; turn the potatoes over and cook for 10 minutes. Turn again and cook for 10 minutes longer or until the potatoes are crispy and tender.

4. Transfer them to a platter and sprinkle with the cheese. Serve immediately.

Serves 4

Little Salads

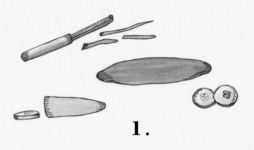

1.

Cucumber Salad

2 large cucumbers, about 1¼ pounds
⅓ cup apple cider vinegar
2 tablespoons orange blossom honey

1. Peel the cucumbers. Slice into very thin
   rounds. Put a colander in the sink and put
   the cucumbers in the colander. Sprinkle
   2 tablespoons salt over the cucumbers and
   toss. Put a plate on top of the cucumbers
   and put a heavy can on the plate. This will
   help release the water from the cucumbers.
   Let sit for 30 minutes. Wash the cucumbers
   thoroughly under cold water to remove
   the salt.

2. Using your hands, squeeze the cucumbers
   to release the water, then put them in a
   bowl. Stir the cider vinegar and honey in a
   cup until honey dissolves. Pour over the
   cucumbers and mix.

3. Add freshly ground black pepper. Cover and
   refrigerate until cold.

Serves 4

2.

Carrot–Pineapple Salad

4 fresh whole carrots, about ½ pound
½ very ripe fresh pineapple
3 tablespoons light mayonnaise

1. Trim the carrots and peel them. Shred the
   carrots on the large holes of a box grater.
   Put the grated carrots in a bowl. Cut the
   pineapple into little cubes (about ¼ inch).
   You will need 6 ounces by weight, or about
   1 cup. Add to the carrots along with any
   pineapple juice that accumulates. Add the
   mayonnaise and stir well.

2. Add salt and freshly ground black pepper
   to taste. Cover and refrigerate for several
   hours, until cold.

Serves 4

3.

Good Potato Salad

4 Yukon Gold potatoes, about 1¼ pounds
1 scallion
⅓ cup light mayonnaise

1. Scrub the potatoes. Put in a large saucepan with cold water to cover by 1 inch. Bring to a boil. Lower the heat to medium and cook for 30 minutes, or until the potatoes are just tender. To see if they're done, poke them with a skewer; if it goes in easily, go on to the next step. Carefully transfer the potatoes to a colander in the sink. Run cold water over the potatoes until they are cool enough to handle.

2. Using your fingers or a small knife, remove the skin from the potatoes and cut them into ½ inch pieces. Place in a bowl. Chop the white part of the scallion very fine to get 1 heaping tablespoon. Add to the potatoes with the mayonnaise and 2 tablespoons water. Stir carefully with a flexible rubber spatula.

3. Add salt and freshly ground black pepper to taste. Serve at room temperature or chilled.

Serves 4

Quick and Healthy Snacks

under 200 calories!

1-2-3 Snacks

Drinks

Fruit and Vegetable Snacks

Savory Breads

Savory Breads

Robyn's Perfect Pitza

Robyn Kimmel, age eight, perfected this delicious snack and had fun testing it many times.

6-inch pita bread
⅔ cup marinara sauce
**½ cup shredded part-skim
mozzarella cheese**

1. Using a small knife, cut the pita bread to separate the bread into 2 circles. If you're not very handy with a knife, just trim away the edges and pull the bread apart to make 2 circles.

2. Toast the pita halves in a toaster oven until crisp and remove carefully. Change the toaster setting to broil. Spread the sauce evenly on the bread halves. Sprinkle with the cheese. Return to the toaster oven to broil for 30 seconds, until golden and bubbly.

Makes 2

EVERY BODY
LOVES PISA...
I MEAN
PIZZA.

"Rozanne let me develop one of the recipes by myself. I made the 'pizza' eight times to get it just right and so now it's called Robyn's Perfect Pitza."

—*Robyn Kimmel, age 8*

Avocado Mash

My mother and I both loved this quick snack, and I was the one who made it for us when I came home from school. The secret is a very ripe avocado because it has a sweet, nutty taste.

¼ small ripe avocado
1 tablespoon Italian dressing
1 slice of white bread

1. Scoop the avocado flesh from the hard skin. Place the avocado on a plate and mash very well with a fork. Add the dressing and mash some more.

2. Spread on the bread to cover completely and sprinkle with salt and freshly ground black pepper. Cut as desired.

Serves 1

Tomato Melt

½ English muffin
1 small ripe tomato
1 slice American cheese

1. Toast the English muffin half in your toaster oven. Remove the English muffin and preheat the toaster oven to 375 degrees. Place the English muffin on a piece of foil.

2. Wash the tomato, pat dry, and slice thin. Place overlapping tomato slices on top of the English muffin half. Sprinkle with salt and pepper. Top with the cheese.

3. Bake for 3-5 minutes, or until the cheese melts and gets a bit browned. Carefully remove and let cool on a plate for 1 minute.

Serves 1

And Ian thought you could only make popcorn in the Microwave!

Ian's Cheese Popcorn

Ian Kimmel, age twelve, tested this recipe several times and was very excited to make popcorn on top of the stove. (He thought you could only make it in a microwave oven!) Ian especially liked shaking the pan and determining it was ready by watching the pot's lid rise a little as the popcorn peeked out.

3 tablespoons olive oil
6 tablespoons popcorn kernels
6 tablespoons grated Parmesan cheese

1. Heat 1 tablespoon of the olive oil in a large saucepan (I use a 3-quart pan) with a cover, swirling the oil so that the bottom of the pan is coated. Add the popcorn, spreading it out to cover the bottom of the pan. Cook over medium heat until the corn begins to pop, then immediately cover the pan. Continue to shake the pan and cook for 3 minutes longer, or until all the popcorn is popped. The cover of the pan will rise a little (the popcorn and steam raise the lid).

2. Transfer the popcorn to a large bowl. While hot, add the remaining 2 tablespoons olive oil and stir. Add the grated cheese and salt to taste. Mix well.

Serves 4 (about 2 cups per serving)

Homemade Pretzel Sticks

These free-form pretzel sticks are fun to make and are extra special when dipped in honey: sweet and salty at the same time!

1 tablespoon granulated yeast
2½ tablespoons honey, plus ¼ cup for dipping
1½ cups all-purpose flour, plus more for kneading

1. Preheat the oven to 400 degrees.

2. Put ½ cup warm tap water in a large bowl. Add the yeast and 1 tablespoon of honey to the warm water, stirring until dissolved. Let sit for 8 minutes, or until the yeast begins to foam.

3. Mix the flour with 1¼ teaspoons salt and add to the yeast mixture. Stir with a long wooden spoon until a crumbly dough forms. Turn the dough out onto a countertop that has been lightly floured. Using clean hands, knead the dough for 5 minutes: Using the heel of one hand, push the top part of the dough away from you. Fold that piece over and push again. Give the dough a one-quarter clockwise turn and repeat until the dough is smooth and no longer sticky. Divide the dough into 6 pieces and roll into long sticks, 8½ inches long and ½ inch wide. Spray a rimmed baking sheet with cooking spray. Put the pretzels on the baking sheet.

4. In a small bowl, mix 1½ tablespoons of the honey with 1 tablespoon of water. Using a pastry brush, brush pretzels lightly with the honey and water mixture. Sprinkle them lightly with Kosher salt. Bake for 18 to 20 minutes or until lightly browned. Let cool. Pour ¼ cup of the remaining honey into a small bowl. Dip the pretzels into the honey.

Makes 6

"The pretzels were very good. They were sweet and crispy. I loved kneading the bread and rolling them out. It was a lot like rolling Play-Doh. It was a lot of fun."

–*Julia Sarah Miller, age 11*

Carrot Sticks with Peanut Butter Dip

Three of my young assistant chefs—Robyn, Ian, and Daniel—invented this dip, which they say tastes like peanut butter cheesecake.

1 large carrot or 10 baby carrots
1½ tablespoons whipped cream cheese
1 tablespoon smooth peanut butter

1. Peel the large carrot and cut into sticks. Or cut baby carrots in half, lengthwise. Put on a plate.

2. In a small bowl, stir together the cream cheese, peanut butter, and 1 tablespoon water until smooth.

3. Add a pinch of salt and stir. Put in a little bowl. Use as a dip for carrots.

Serves 1

Grape Tomato Skewers with Pesto Dip

You will need eight long frilly toothpicks.

8 cherry tomatoes or grape tomatoes
¼ cup plain yogurt
1 tablespoon pesto

1. Wash the tomatoes and dry them with a paper towel. Spear each tomato with a toothpick. Place on a plate.

2. In a small bowl mix the yogurt and pesto thoroughly. Add salt and pepper to taste.

3. Place in a small bowl and dunk the tomatoes.

Serves 1

Cinnamon Oodles

Here's something different to whip up any day. It's a treat I loved as a kid. You can buy cinnamon-sugar in a jar or simply make your own (see page 42).

1½ ounces dried wide egg noodles
1 teaspoon unsalted butter
1 teaspoon cinnamon-sugar

1. Bring a large saucepan of salted water to a boil. Add the egg noodles and cook until tender, about 8 minutes.

2. Drain the noodles well in a colander. Transfer to a flat soup bowl and toss with the butter. Add salt to taste. Sprinkle with the cinnamon-sugar and serve immediately.

Serves 1

Scrumptious Stuffed Eggs

Make these in the morning before you leave for school. The secret here is pickle relish. You may use sweet relish, or India relish (which is spicier and exotic), or hot-dog relish that has been mixed with mustard.

4 hard-boiled eggs (see page 30)
2 tablespoons light mayonnaise
3 tablespoons pickle relish

1. Peel the eggs and cut them in half lengthwise. Remove the yolks and place them in a bowl. Mix in the mayonnaise and mash with a fork until creamy. Add half of the relish and stir. Add salt and pepper to taste.

2. Using a spoon, fill the cavities of the egg halves with yolk mixture. Dab with a bit of remaining relish. Cover and chill until ready to serve.

Makes 8 halves

These eggs are straight
from Heaven.

Apple Wedges with...

1 medium apple

with...

2 teaspoons peanut butter
2 teaspoons sprinkles (chocolate or rainbow)

or...

2 teaspoons peanut butter
2 teaspoons real maple syrup

or...

1 tablespoon honey
1 tablespoon chopped dry-roasted peanuts

or...

1 tablespoon honey
½ ounce crushed pretzels

or...

1½ tablespoons real maple syrup
1 tablespoon toasted sesame seeds

1. Wash the apple and dry it well. Cut the apple into 6 or 8 wedges. Choose any of the options above for a healthy snack.

2. Using a butter knife, spread the peanut butter on apple wedges and top with sprinkles or drizzle with maple syrup. Or drizzle honey or maple syrup over apple wedges and top with peanuts, pretzels, or sesame seeds.

Serves 1

Roasted Bananas

When you put bananas in a hot oven, the skin turns black but the flesh becomes soft and sweet. You eat the banana with a spoon. A wonderful variation was created by Daniel Glass, age eleven (see right).

2 ripe medium-size bananas in their skins
2 teaspoons sugar
2 teaspoons chocolate sprinkles

1. Preheat the oven to 450 degrees.

2. Put the bananas on a rack in the oven. Bake for 20 minutes. Remove the bananas. Carefully peel off one strip of skin on the inner curve of each hot banana. Put each banana on a plate.

3. Sprinkle each banana with 1 teaspoon of sugar and 1 teaspoon of chocolate sprinkles and eat with a spoon.

Serves 2

"It was so much fun to roast the bananas and eat the insides with a spoon. I invented a version of my own: Place chocolate chips on the hot banana, wait one minute until the chocolate melts, and sprinkle with flaked coconut. Yum!"
–Daniel Glass, age 11

Daniel's Variation

1. Roast the **bananas** as directed. Place 2 teaspoons of **chocolate chips** in each hot banana. Wait for 1 minute, until the chocolate melts, and sprinkle each with 2 teaspoons of flaked (sweetened) **coconut**.

Fresh Fruit Smoothies

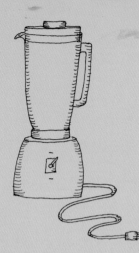

Pineapple–Mango Smoothie

1 pound fresh pineapple chunks
1 ripe mango
2 cups vanilla soy milk, chilled

1. Put the pineapple chunks in the freezer for several hours until hard. When ready to serve, remove the skin from the mango using a small, sharp knife. Cut away the mango flesh from the pit and cut into chunks.

2. Place the mango in a blender. Add the soy milk and frozen pineapple chunks. Process on high for two minutes, or longer, until very smooth. Serve immediately in tumblers or wine glasses.

Serves 4

Blueberry–Banana Smoothie

1 cup fresh or frozen blueberries
1 very ripe banana
8 ounces vanilla yogurt

1. If using fresh berries, wash them and pat dry. Put in the freezer for several hours until frozen. (You can do this before you go to school.) Put the frozen berries in a blender.

2. Slice the banana and add to the blender. Add the yogurt, 8 ice cubes, and ¼ cup cold water. Process on high until very smooth, thick, and creamy. Add a little more water if necessary.

Serves 2

Strawberry–Coconut Smoothie

This is a super-duper drink! The color looks like bubble gum and it thickens as it sits in the fridge.

**8 ounces ripe strawberries,
plus two small berries for garnishing
1 cup light coconut milk
2½ tablespoons sugar**

1. Wash the berries and pat dry. Remove the stems from all but the two berries for garnishing. Cut the remaining berries into thick slices. You will have 1 packed cup.

2. Put the berries in a blender. Add the coconut milk, sugar, and 8 large ice cubes. Blend until the mixture is very smooth and thick. Serve immediately in 2 chilled glasses or refrigerate until very cold. The mixture will thicken as it sits.

3. Garnish each glass with a whole berry.

Serves 2

Dinner Is Fun

Dinner is easy to prepare. As a first course you can have a soup, salad, shrimp cocktail, or a half-portion of pasta. Your main course should include a protein (fish, chicken, pork, lamb, or beef) and a side dish or two.

Vegetarians might have a full order of pasta, and everyone will find a rainbow of ideas in the Vegetables and Side Dishes chapter (page 104). Keep it simple during the week and make it more elaborate on the weekend when you have more time to cook—and eat!

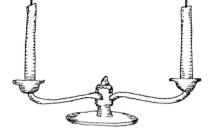

Light-as-a-Feather Soup

Yep, it looks like there are lots of feathers in this bowl of soup! In Italy, it is called stracciatella *and its third ingredient is Parmesan cheese, which gets sprinkled on top. In China, the soup is known as egg-drop soup and you add soy sauce at the end instead of the cheese. Either way, it's light as a feather.*

2 cups good-quality chicken broth

2 extra-large eggs

**¼ cup freshly grated Parmesan cheese
or 2 teaspoons soy sauce**

1. Put the chicken broth in a small saucepan. Bring to a boil. Lower the heat to a simmer. Simmer for 5 minutes. Add a generous grinding of black pepper.

2. Break the eggs into a bowl and, using a fork, beat vigorously until well blended. Pour the beaten eggs into the soup and stir with a fork to make feathery ribbons of egg. Cook for 2 minutes, until the egg is just firm. Pour the soup into 2 bowls.

3. Top each bowl of soup with Parmesan cheese or stir in soy sauce. Serve immediately.

Serves 2

"Light-as-a-Feather Soup tastes just like 'take-out soup' at home!"
–Rachel Greenberg, age 12

Green-as-Grass
Spinach Soup

The title says it all! You can top the soup with croutons or grated cheese or a chopped hard-boiled egg.

2 large white potatoes, about 1 pound

9 ounces fresh baby spinach, prewashed, about 5 packed cups

5 tablespoons unsalted butter

1. Peel the potatoes and cut into 1-inch chunks. Put the potatoes in a 4-quart pot with 8 cups of water and 1 teaspoon of salt. Bring to a rapid boil. Lower the heat to medium and cook for 15 minutes, or until the potatoes become tender. The tines of a fork should go in easily.

2. Add the spinach and continue to cook for 5 minutes. The potatoes will be soft and the spinach should still be bright green.

3. **Ask an adult to help you with the next steps.** Using a slotted spoon, transfer the potatoes and spinach to the bowl of a food processor. Keep 2 cups of the cooking liquid. Process until the potatoes and spinach are blended. Slowly add the 2 cups of cooking liquid until smooth and thick. Slice the butter and add to the soup. Process until very smooth. Add salt and pepper to taste. Reheat before serving.

Serves 4 or more

Quick "French Dressing"

Here's a great dressing you can make in a snap.

⅓ cup ketchup

2 tablespoons yellow mustard

1½ tablespoons honey

1. Mix in a small bowl until well blended.

Mixed Green Salad with Raspberry Dressing

You can buy your favorite prewashed mixed greens in any supermarket, from "spring mix" to "field greens." White balsamic vinegar can be used instead of raspberry.

1 tablespoon raspberry vinegar

¼ cup olive oil

4 ounces mixed greens, about 4 packed cups, chilled

1. Put the raspberry vinegar in a cup. Using a fork, slowly whisk in the olive oil until blended. The dressing will "emulsify" or thicken.

2. Wash the greens, if necessary, and dry well using paper towels or a salad spinner, which is lots of fun to use. Put the greens in a large bowl. Pour the dressing over the greens. Toss well. Add salt and freshly ground black pepper to taste. Serve immediately.

Serves 4

Iceberg Salad with Blue Cheese and Bacon

Fun iceberg tip: Slam the bottom of the head on a wooden board and the core will simply fall out! Or ask an adult for some help.

6 ounces mild blue cheese (about 1 cup)
8 slices bacon
1 large head of iceberg lettuce

1. Crumble the cheese into small pieces. You will have a heaping cup. Put all but ¼ cup of the cheese in the bowl of a food processor. Process the cheese while you slowly add ½ cup cold water, a little at a time. Blend until completely smooth. Transfer to a bowl. The dressing will thicken as it sits. Cover and refrigerate until cold. Add a little more water if the dressing is too thick.

2. Cook the bacon in a large nonstick skillet on medium heat until just crispy. Transfer to paper towels to drain.

3. Cut the lettuce into 6 wedges. Put 1 wedge on each of 6 plates. Spoon dressing over the lettuce and crumble bacon on top. Sprinkle with a little of the remaining crumbled cheese.

Serves 6

BACON

Bowties with Broccoli

This is a two-in-one recipe because the broccoli florets are tossed with the pasta while the broccoli stems become a buttery sauce! I like to use bowtie-shaped pasta (known as farfalle *in Italian). But there are hundreds of shapes to choose from.*

1 very large head of broccoli
3 tablespoons unsalted butter, chilled
8 ounces bowtie pasta

1. Cut off all the florets from the head of broccoli, leaving their stems ½ inch long. Cut these pieces in half lengthwise and set aside.

2. Using a vegetable peeler, peel the long stems and discard the peelings. Cut the peeled stems into 1-inch pieces. Put the stems in a small saucepan with 1¼ cups water. Bring to a boil. Lower the heat to a simmer, cover the pot, and cook until the broccoli is very soft, about 15 minutes. Let cool for 5 minutes.

3. **With the help of an adult,** transfer the cooked broccoli stems and cooking liquid to a blender. Process until smooth. Add small bits of butter and process again until very smooth and creamy. Add a little water if the sauce is too thick. Add salt and pepper to taste. Transfer the sauce to a small saucepan and reheat when the pasta is almost cooked (see next step).

4. Meanwhile, bring a large pot of salted water to a boil. Add the pasta and cook for 8 minutes. Add the halved broccoli florets and cook for 5 minutes longer, or until the pasta and broccoli are tender. Do not overcook; you want the broccoli to be bright green. Drain well in a colander. Divide the pasta with broccoli among 4 bowls. Pour the hot sauce over the top and serve immediately.

Optional garnish: Top with a curlicue of chilled butter before serving. Use a vegetable peeler and slide it over a stick of butter to make paper-thin curls.

Serves 4

You can wear a bowtie to dinner,
or you can eat a plate of them.

White-and-Green Pasta in Pink Sauce

Fettuccine comes packaged with both white and green noodles and looks really neat swimming in a puddle of pink sauce. There are lots of different tomato sauces available; you can use one flavored with roasted garlic or herbs, if you wish.

8 ounces white-and-green fettuccine
1 cup tomato sauce
⅔ cup light cream

1. Bring a large pot of salted water to a boil. Add the pasta and cook for 10 to 12 minutes if using dried pasta, or 4 to 5 minutes if using fresh. Do not overcook as you don't want the pasta to be mushy.

2. Meanwhile, put the tomato sauce and cream in a small saucepan. Cook over medium-high heat, whisking with a wire whisk until smooth and hot. Add salt to taste.

3. When the pasta is done, drain in a colander set in the sink. Shake off all the water and transfer the pasta to 4 warm bowls. Spoon hot sauce over the pasta and serve immediately. Pass the peppermill at the table.

Serves 4

Pineapple-Glazed
Salmon Steaks

Salmon steaks are cut across the width of the fish into portions with a small bone in the center. Pineapple juice and soy sauce make a magical glaze.

2 cups unsweetened pineapple juice
4 teaspoons soy sauce
4 6-ounce salmon steaks

1. Put the pineapple juice in a small saucepan. (Do not use aluminum because it will create an undesirable chemical reaction.) Bring to a boil. Lower the heat to medium and cook until the juice is reduced to 1 cup. Remove from the heat and cool. Stir in the soy sauce.

2. Place the salmon in a shallow casserole. Pour the pineapple–soy mixture over the fish. Add a grinding of black pepper. Refrigerate for 2 hours, turning the fish after the first hour.

3. Place in a very large nonstick sauté pan (I use a 12-inch pan) over medium heat until hot. Add the salmon and cook for 3 minutes. Using a spatula, carefully turn the fish over and cook for 3 to 4 minutes, until just cooked through. Do not overcook.

4. Meanwhile, put the remaining pineapple–soy mixture into a small skillet. Cook over high heat until reduced by half, about 5 minutes. Using a pastry brush, brush the top of the salmon with some of the reduced marinade. Remove the fish from the pan and serve.

Serves 4

1.

2.

3.

Shrimp Cocktail with Tomato Sorbet

The best way to cook shrimp? Salt the cooking water until it tastes like the ocean. It is great fun to dunk the cooked shrimp into the slushy cocktail "sorbet."

1 cup cocktail sauce
3 lemons
1 pound very large shrimp (in their shells)

1. Put the cocktail sauce into a small bowl. Using the fine holes of a box grater, or a Microplane, grate the zest of 1 lemon. Be careful not to include any of the bitter white pith. Add the grated zest to the cocktail sauce. Squeeze the lemon to get 2 tablespoons of juice. Add to the bowl and stir. Place the bowl in the freezer and stir every 30 minutes until a firm but slushy texture forms, about 2 hours.

2. Wash the shrimp in cold water. Bring a medium pot of water to a rapid boil. Add ⅓ cup kosher salt or more—so that the water tastes as salty as the ocean. Add the shrimp and lower the heat to medium. Cook for 3 to 4 minutes, until the shrimp are just pink and firm. Drain the shrimp and put them in a bowl of heavily salted ice-cold water for 10 minutes.

3. Peel the shrimp, leaving the tails intact. Cut the remaining 2 lemons in half across the width to get four halves. Slice ¼ inch or so off from the bottom of each half so that it sits upright without wobbling. Scoop out the flesh and discard. Using a small ice cream scoop, put tomato "sorbet" into each lemon cup, mounding up high. Put a lemon cup in the center of each of 4 plates. Surround with shrimp and serve immediately.

Serves 4

Fillet of Flounder
with Lemon Butter

You can use fillets of sole instead of flounder, and fresh lime instead of lemon!

4 6-ounce flounder fillets, skin removed
6 tablespoons (¾ stick) unsalted butter, chilled
2 large lemons

1. Season the fish with salt and pepper. Melt 3 tablespoons of the butter in a very large nonstick skillet. Cook the fish over high heat until golden and slightly crispy, about 3 minutes on each side. When cooked to desired doneness, transfer the fish using a spatula to a warm platter. Cover with foil.

2. Add the juice of 1 lemon to the pan and let the sauce bubble up. Cook until the butter is nut-colored, or light brown: Be careful not to burn it. Remove from the heat and add the remaining 3 tablespoons of chilled butter. Swirl the pan until the butter melts. Heat briefly, adding salt and pepper to taste. Pour the sauce over the fish. Top with very thin slices of the remaining lemon, if desired.

Serves 4

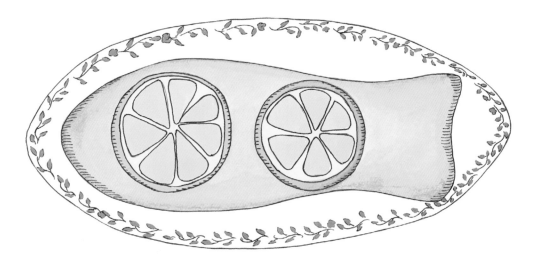

Quick 1-2-3 Gravy

1. Pour 1 cup of water into the roasting pan and scrape up the browned bits.

2. Pour through a fine strainer into a small saucepan.

3. Bring to a boil and cook over high heat until the juices thicken.

4. If using butter, add a tablespoon of cold butter to enrich the sauce. You can add some finely chopped thyme or a squeeze of the cooked lemon to the sauce.

A Simple Roast Chicken

Every kid should know how to make a simple roast chicken. Flavor it with fresh thyme or a lemon. Baste it with melted butter or olive oil. Delicious every way.

4-pound roasting chicken

1 bunch of fresh thyme or a lemon, pierced several times with a fork

4 tablespoons melted butter or olive oil

1. Preheat the oven to 350 degrees.

2. Remove the giblets from the cavity of the chicken and discard. Wash the chicken and dry well. Fill the cavity with the fresh thyme or with the lemon. With kitchen string, tie the legs together. Tuck the wings under the chicken. Put the chicken on a rack on a rimmed baking sheet. Rub salt all over the chicken. Drizzle with half of the melted butter or olive oil. Roast for about 1 hour and 10 minutes, basting several times during roasting with the remaining butter or oil.

3. When the chicken is done, remove it from the oven. Transfer the chicken to a cutting board and sprinkle with salt and freshly ground black pepper. Let the chicken rest for 5 minutes. Remove the thyme or lemon. Carve the chicken as desired, **asking your kitchen buddy to help.**

Serves 6

"A simple roast chicken is something every kid should know how to make. You can do it your way. With olive oil or butter, and then flavor it with fresh thyme, lemon, or garlic. Using butter and garlic is my favorite way."

—*Danielle Hartog, age 11*

Ketchup–Cola Chicken

Finger-licking good, this is great hot, cold, or in between. You can substitute root beer if you'd like.

1 cup ketchup
1 cup Pepsi, Coke, or other cola
3½-pound chicken, quartered

1. Preheat the oven to 350 degrees.

2. In a large bowl, whisk together the ketchup and cola until thoroughly mixed. Wash the chicken and pat dry with paper towels. Remove the wings from the chicken breast quarters. Put all of the chicken pieces in the bowl and toss so that the chicken is coated with the ketchup–cola mixture. Let sit for 30 minutes or, refrigerated, up to 8 hours.

3. Remove the chicken, reserving the marinade. Place the chicken, skin side up, on a rimmed baking sheet. Sprinkle the chicken with salt and and freshly ground black pepper. Bake for 1 hour. Meanwhile, put the marinade in a small saucepan and bring to a boil. Reduce the heat to medium and cook until the marinade is reduced to 1 cup, about 15 minutes. During baking, baste the chicken with the reduced marinade several times, using a pastry brush. After 30 minutes, **have an adult help you** transfer the chicken to a plate, pour off the fat, and return the chicken to the pan. Continue cooking for 30 minutes.

4. When the chicken is done, transfer it to a warm platter. Drizzle with a little more warm marinade, serving any extra on the side.

Serves 4

Three-Minute Chicken

This looks like a big open-face melted ham-and-cheese sand-wich. But instead of the bread there's a nice chicken cutlet! You assemble it in three minutes, then bake it for twelve.

4 very thin chicken cutlets
4 slices of boiled ham, ¾ ounce each
4 slices of Swiss cheese, I ounce each

1. Preheat the oven to 375 degrees.

2. Spray a rimmed baking sheet with cooking spray or line with foil. Sprinkle lightly with salt and pepper.

3. Place the chicken cutlets on a baking sheet, several inches apart. Place a piece of ham on each piece of chicken. Place a slice of cheese on the ham. Bake for 12 minutes, or until the cheese is melted (but not running all over the baking pan) and the chicken is cooked through—no pink! Do not overcook. Serve immediately with a colorful side dish.

Serves 4

What Are
Chicken Cutlets?

Chicken cutlets are cut from skinless, boneless chicken breasts into large, very thin slices. They are often packaged as "cutlets." To prepare your own, with an adult, carefully cut large skinless, boneless chicken breasts in half as though you were slicing a bagel.

Rosemary Meatballs

It's amazing how moist low-fat turkey can taste, provided you don't overcook the meatballs. All my young friends love them.

8 ounces ground turkey
1 small onion
2 branches of fresh rosemary

1. Put the turkey in a medium bowl. Peel the onion and cut it in half. Grate the onion on the large holes of a box grater to get 2 tablespoons grated onion juice and pulp. Add to the turkey.

2. Remove the leaves from 1 rosemary branch and chop as fine as possible to get 1 teaspoon minced rosemary. Add a little less than ½ teaspoon salt and ¼ teaspoon freshly ground black pepper. Mix until all the ingredients are blended. Form the mixture into 16 balls.

3. Heat a large nonstick skillet until hot. Add the meatballs and cook for 2 minutes over high heat; lower the heat to medium and roll the meatballs around the pan so they don't stick. Cook for 3 to 4 minutes longer, until just firm. Do not overcook. Serve immediately, garnished with fresh rosemary sprigs.

Makes 16 (serves 2 or 3)

Chicken Ooh-la-la

Boursin cheese, imported from France, is something I've loved since I was a kid. It's flavored with herbs and garlic and is smooth and creamy. You can substitute fresh herbed goat cheese. Make this recipe with a crust of finely chopped pecans or a sheer layer of orange marmalade. Either way it's ooh-la-la.

1 package Boursin cheese, 5.2 ounces

4 large skinless, boneless chicken breasts

¾ cup chopped pecans

or

4 tablespoons orange marmalade

1. Let the cheese come to room temperature. Preheat the oven to 350 degrees.

2. Using a butter knife, spread the cheese on each breast to completely cover.

3. If using pecans, chop them very fine. Sprinkle 3 tablespoons of pecans evenly over each breast and pat in lightly. Or, using a butter knife, spread 1 tablespoon of marmalade on each breast to coat cheese lightly and evenly.

4. Spray a rimmed baking sheet with cooking spray or line with foil. Put the chicken breasts on the baking sheet several inches apart. Bake for 25 minutes. Do not overcook. Serve immediately.

Serves 4

Great 1-2-3 Idea

To Make Scallion Brushes:

1. Remove the dark green parts from 8 scallions, leaving only 2 to 3 inches of the light green part.

2. Cut off the root ends to make them even.

3. Make 1 to 2-inch slits up from the white part of the scallion toward the darker end, as if cutting them into quarters, leaving 1 inch uncut at the light green top.

4. Put them in a deep bowl of cold water.

5. Cover and refrigerate for 2 hours, or until the scallions curl up into little brushes.

Makes 8

Very Good Meatballs

These are very easy to make. And you can garnish them with cool-looking scallion "brushes." Instead of making meatballs, you can also form the mixture into four big oval "chopped steaks" and broil them.

2 bunches of scallions
1½ pounds ground beef
3 tablespoons teriyaki sauce

1. Wash the scallions. Cut off the dark green parts of the scallions and discard. Chop enough of the white parts of the scallions to get ¼ cup finely chopped.

2. Place the meat in a large bowl. Add the chopped scallions, 2 tablespoons of the teriyaki sauce, ½ teaspoon salt, and freshly ground black pepper. Using clean hands, combine the ingredients thoroughly. Form into 24 meatballs that are about 1½ inches in diameter.

3. Heat a very large nonstick sauté pan (I use a 12-inch pan) until hot. Add the meatballs and cook over high heat for several minutes, rolling the meatballs around so they brown and become a little crispy on all sides, about 10 minutes. Using a slotted spoon, place the meatballs on a platter and sprinkle with the remaining teriyaki sauce.

Makes 24

Throw a party and serve
these festive meatballs!

Pork Chops
with Sautéed Apples

This is an adaptation of a simple French recipe that any kid can make. McIntosh apples sautéed in butter taste better than pie. Rib chops, not loin chops, are best for this dish.

2 thick pork chops, about 7 ounces each
1 large McIntosh apple
2 tablespoons unsalted butter

1. Season the pork chops with salt and freshly ground black pepper.

2. Peel the apple. Cut the apple in half. Cut each half into 5 wedges. Remove the seeds.

3. Melt the butter in a large (I use a 10-inch) skillet. Add the apples and cook over medium-high heat for 1 minute on each side. Add the pork chops and cook for 4 minutes. Turn the pork chops and apple wedges over. The butter will turn brown (do not let it turn black): This is known as brown butter or *beurre noisette* in French. Cook for 3 to 4 minutes longer, until just firm. Do not overcook or the pork will get dry.

4. Remove the pork chops and apples from the pan. Serve immediately.

Serves 2

Juicy Pork with Prunes

Prunes are now known by another name—dried plums—which, in case you were wondering, is what they are! This is a beautiful and delicious dish to share with friends. Make sure the cheese is grated (like sand), not shredded.

14-ounce pork tenderloin

10 small pitted prunes

⅓ cup freshly grated Asiago cheese

1. Preheat the oven to 375 degrees.

2. Cut a 1-inch-deep slit down the entire length of the tenderloin, leaving 1 inch on each end uncut. The idea is to make a deep channel in the tenderloin so that you can stuff it with prunes.

3. Place the prunes side by side in the channel and sprinkle with all but 1 tablespoon of the cheese. Cut 8 6-inch pieces of string. Tie the tenderloin at 1½-inch intervals, pulling tight so that the prunes are covered. Season the pork with salt and freshly ground black pepper.

4. Spray a rimmed baking sheet with cooking spray. Put the tenderloin on the baking sheet and dust with the remaining cheese. Bake for 20 minutes. Remove from the oven. Let the pork rest for 5 minutes. Cut into ½-inch-thick slices and discard string. Serve immediately.

Serves 4

A Rainbow of Vegetables and Side Dishes

"The vegetable chapter is my favorite! I loved the Green Beans with Pesto and Walnuts and the 'Creamed' Spinach. I brought it to school for lunch, and now I want to bring it every day!"

–Danielle Hartog, age 11

Nutritionists say, "You should eat all the colors to be as healthy as can be." The colors of the rainbow spell ROYGBIV: red, orange, yellow, green, blue, indigo, violet. I learned that when I was a kid and never forgot it. There aren't too many veggies that are blue, indigo, or violet. Can you think of any? (Hint: eggplant, blue potatoes from Peru, blue corn, purple bell peppers.) Don't forget white veggies, too. Can you think of any?

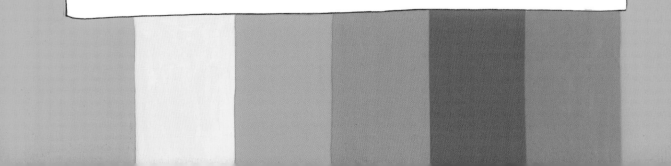

Carrots,
three ways

Simple

Glazed Carrot Coins

This technique produces a lovely glaze for the carrots. Instead of parsley, you might use a sprinkling of grated lemon zest or nutmeg.

1 pound carrots
1½ tablespoons butter
**3 tablespoons chopped
flat-leaf parsley**

1. Peel the carrots and cut them into thin round slices, about ⅛ inch thick. Put them in a 3-quart saucepan. Add 1 cup of water and ¼ teaspoon salt. Slice the butter and scatter on top. Bring to a boil. Cover the pot and reduce the heat to medium-high. Cook for 10 minutes and then uncover. Cook for a few minutes longer, until the carrots are tender.

2. Using a slotted spoon, transfer the carrots to a heat-proof bowl. Reduce the liquid in the pan until it is thick and syrupy, and pour it over the carrots. Toss with salt and freshly ground black pepper. Sprinkle with the parsley.

Serves 4

Fun

Carrot "Fries" with Mint

With a simple kitchen tool that cuts potatoes into crinkly French fries, you can cut carrots into similar shapes. Or cut them with a knife with the help of your kitchen buddy. Fresh basil may be substituted for the mint.

1 pound long slender carrots

3 tablespoons olive oil

1 bunch of fresh mint

1. Preheat the oven to 375 degrees.

2. Peel the carrots. Using a crinkle cutter or a large knife, cut the carrots in half across the width. Cut the slender half lengthwise into 2 long pieces. Cut the thicker half lengthwise into 4 long pieces: The goal is to get carrot sticks shaped like French fries.

3. Put the carrots on a rimmed baking sheet. Drizzle with the oil. Using clean hands, toss the carrots so that they are completely coated with oil. Sprinkle with salt and freshly ground black pepper. Roast for 20 to 25 minutes, until tender, turning the carrots once or twice during baking. The carrots will be golden brown. Transfer to a platter.

4. Wash the mint (or basil) and dry well. Cut into very thin strips to get 2 tablespoons. Scatter over the carrots.

Serves 4

Divine

Baby Carrots with Sweet Garlic

You will be surprised how sweet the garlic becomes when it is cooked long and s-l-o-w-l-y.

1 pound baby carrots

10 small garlic cloves

3 tablespoons olive oil

1. Place the carrots in a 4-quart saucepan.

2. Peel the garlic and cut in half lengthwise. Add to the carrots. Add the olive oil and ⅔ cup water. Add ½ teaspoon salt and bring to a boil. Reduce the heat to very low and cover the pot. Simmer for 30 minutes, or until the carrots are tender, stirring several times during cooking.

3. With a slotted spoon, transfer the carrots and garlic to a bowl. Cook the pan juices over high heat until thick and syrupy, about 5 minutes. Toss with the carrots, adding salt and freshly ground black pepper to taste.

Serves 4

Corn-on-the-Cob with Honey Butter

Few vegetables are more fun to eat than corn-on-the-cob, especially when it's slathered with sweet honey butter that drips down your chin! Break the cobs in half with your hands to make "mini corns."

2 large ears of corn

4 tablespoons (½ stick) unsalted butter, at room temperature

1 tablespoon honey

1. Put the butter in the bowl of an electric mixer or simply put in a bowl. Add the honey and a pinch of salt. Beat with the electric mixer until smooth and creamy, or mash the butter and honey together until thoroughly blended. Set aside.

2. Remove the husk (that's the green outer leaves) and silk (those are the long, golden threads under the husk) from the corn. Place both hands firmly on each cob and break in half, as evenly as possible, to get 2 smaller pieces.

3. Bring a medium saucepan of water to a boil. Add the corn and lower the heat to medium. Cover the saucepan and cook the corn for about 8 minutes.

4. Using tongs, transfer the corn to a platter. Sprinkle lightly with salt. Top with the honey butter and serve immediately.

Serves 4

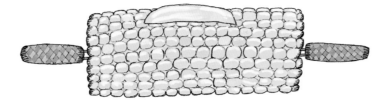

Cauliflower "Popcorn"

Roasting small cauliflower florets turns them into yielding, golden nuggets that become addictive when topped with sharp cheddar. One-half cup of freshly grated Parmesan can be substituted.

1 large head of cauliflower
3 tablespoons extra-virgin olive oil
1 cup shredded sharp white cheddar cheese, about 3 ounces

1. Preheat the oven to 400 degrees.

2. Cut the cauliflower in half. Remove the core with a small knife and discard. Break the head into small florets, about ¾-inch pieces. Place in a bowl. Toss with the olive oil and sprinkle with salt and pepper. Place on a rimmed baking sheet and roast for 35 to 40 minutes, until soft and caramelized (they will turn golden brown), turning once during cooking. Shake the pan gently several times during baking so that the cauliflower doesn't stick.

3. Transfer the cooked cauliflower to a platter. Add salt and freshly ground black pepper and sprinkle with the cheese. Serve hot or at room temperature.

Serves 4

Cauliflower with Garlicky Bread Crumbs

1. Break **1 large head of cauliflower** into large florets. Boil in salted water for 15 minutes, or until tender. Drain well in a colander.

2. Meanwhile, put **1 tablespoon of garlic oil** in a small skillet. Add **½ cup seasoned bread crumbs**. Cook for several minutes, stirring constantly, until the crumbs are crispy. Add salt and freshly ground black pepper to taste.

3. Drizzle several tablespoons of garlic oil over the hot cauliflower and scatter the bread crumbs on top.

Serves 4

Chinese-style

Asparagus-in-a-Wok

It is best to use slender asparagus, sometimes known as "pencil" asparagus. This way the dish can be stir-fried in less than five minutes.

1¼ pounds slender asparagus

**1 large red, yellow, or
orange bell pepper**

**1 tablespoon garlic oil
(or extra-virgin olive oil)**

1. Snap off the woody bottoms of the asparagus, then trim the stalks to equal length. Cut each asparagus stalk on the bias into 2-inch pieces. ("On the bias" means that instead of cutting straight across each stalk, you cut at an angle.)

2. Cut off the panels (the 4 sides) of the bell pepper to get 4 rectangular shapes. Remove the seeds, then cut the panels into strips that are about 2 inches long and ⅛ inch wide.

3. Heat the oil in a wok or large sauté pan. Add the asparagus and pepper strips. Stir-fry over medium-high heat, tossing constantly, until the asparagus begin to brown, about 3 minutes. Add 1 tablespoon of water and continue to cook, stirring constantly, until tender but still a little crunchy. Toss with salt and freshly ground black pepper.

Serves 4

Steamed Broccoli with Stir-Fried Pecans

You can cut the florets from a large head of broccoli or simply buy one pound of florets. This is the best way imaginable to get anyone to eat broccoli.

1 large bunch of broccoli

½ cup coarsely chopped pecans

3 tablespoons teriyaki sauce

1. Cut the broccoli into large florets, leaving 1½ inches of the stem attached. (You will have about 1 pound of florets.) Place the broccoli in a steamer basket and steam, covered, over boiling water for about 8 minutes, until soft but still bright green.

2. Meanwhile, toast the pecans in a small nonstick skillet over medium heat. Stir them constantly until toasted (dark brown), being careful not to let them burn.

3. In a large bowl, toss the hot broccoli with the toasted pecans and teriyaki sauce. Season with salt and freshly ground black pepper. Serve immediately.

Serves 4

Chinese-style

Snow Peas and Baby Corn

I loved to eat miniature baby corn as a kid. It is available in cans or jars in the Asian section of most supermarkets, and it's delicious and colorful paired with crunchy snow peas. Asian sesame oil is available in the same aisle as the baby corn.

1 pound fresh snow peas
15-ounce can whole baby corn
1½ tablespoons Asian sesame oil

1. Wash the snow peas. Pat dry. Trim the ends and remove the strings running along the side.

2. Place the corn in a colander and wash under cold water. Pat dry.

3. Put the snow peas and corn in a steamer basket and carefully set the basket over a pot of boiling water.

4. Cover and cook for 8 minutes, or until the snow peas are tender but still bright green. Transfer to a bowl and toss with the sesame oil. Add salt and freshly ground black pepper to taste.

Serves 4

"I made the snow peas and baby corn totally on my own. The sesame oil gave the vegetables a really yummy taste. My little sister loved the corn and so did I."

–Danielle Hartog, age 11

Broccoli Spears with Cheese Sauce

This sauce is sooo easy to make and it looks just like a classic French cream sauce known as mornay. *The cheese should be grated on the small holes of your grater so that it looks like sand (not shredded).*

2 thick broccoli spears, about ½ head

⅓ cup milk

½ cup grated Parmesan cheese

1. Place the broccoli spears in a saucepan large enough to hold them without overlapping. Cover with enough water to come almost to the top of the broccoli. Add ½ teaspoon salt and bring to a full boil. Cover the saucepan and lower the heat to medium-high. Cook for 12 minutes or until tender, but do not overcook. The broccoli should still be bright green.

2. Meanwhile, in a small saucepan, put the milk and 5 tablespoons of the Parmesan cheese. Cook over medium heat, stirring constantly with a wooden spoon, until the sauce thickens and you see the first bubbles. Lower the heat and simmer for several minutes until the sauce thickens and lightly coats the wooden spoon. Add salt and pepper to taste.

3. Drain the broccoli well and place on a small platter. Pour the hot cheese sauce over the broccoli and sprinkle with the remaining grated cheese. Pass the peppermill.

Serves 2

"Creamed" Spinach

There is no cream in this dish; instead, the wonderfully creamy
texture comes from puréed cottage cheese. No one will know!
Frozen spinach works especially well in this recipe.

2 packages frozen leaf spinach (10 ounces each)
1¼ cups low-fat cottage cheese
2½ tablespoons unsalted butter

1. In a large saucepan with a cover, combine ½ cup water and
   ½ teaspoon salt and bring to a boil. Add the frozen spinach
   and bring to a boil. Cover and reduce the heat to medium-
   high. Cook for 10 minutes, stirring several times. Spinach
   should still be bright green. Drain thoroughly in a colander
   set in the sink. Make sure to shake out all the water. Pat the
   spinach dry with paper towels.

2. Transfer the hot spinach to a food processor. Add the cottage
   cheese and all but 1 teaspoon of the butter. Process until
   very smooth. Return to the saucepan and add salt and freshly
   ground black pepper to taste. Heat gently and transfer to
   a warm bowl. Top with the remaining teaspoon of butter.
   Serve immediately.

Serves 4

Green Beans,
three ways

Simple

Green Beans Almondine

A simple dish that's loved by all.

1 pound green beans
2 tablespoons unsalted butter
3 tablespoons sliced almonds

1. Wash the beans and trim the ends. Using a small, sharp knife, cut the beans in thirds across the width. You may also leave the beans whole.

2. Choose a saucepan large enough to hold the beans comfortably. Add enough water to fill it by two-thirds and bring the water to a boil with a teaspoon of salt. Add the beans and cook for 3 to 4 minutes if you've cut them, and 5 to 6 minutes if you've left them whole. Drain them immediately into a colander. Pat dry with a paper towel.

3. Put the butter into the saucepan in which the beans were cooked and melt the butter over medium heat. Add the almonds and cook just until they take on some color, about 2 minutes. Then add the drained beans and ½ teaspoon of salt, and cook for about 2 minutes, tossing until the beans are coated with butter. Add freshly ground black pepper and serve.

Serves 4 or more

Fun

Green Beans with Pesto and Walnuts

This is great to take to a picnic or pack in a lunch box.

1 pound green beans
⅔ cup coarsely chopped walnut pieces
¼ cup good-quality prepared pesto

1. Trim the ends of the beans with a small, sharp knife. Cut the beans in half through the width. Set aside.

2. Bring a large pot of water, fitted with a steamer basket, to a boil. Place the beans in the steamer basket and cover the pot. Steam for about 6 minutes, until the beans are tender but still bright green.

3. Put the walnuts in a small nonstick skillet over medium-high heat, stirring constantly, until the nuts are lightly toasted, about 2 minutes. Sprinkle lightly with salt and set aside.

4. Put the pesto in a medium bowl. When the beans are cooked, shake off any extra moisture and add the beans to the bowl with the pesto. Toss quickly and add the nuts. Add salt and freshly ground black pepper to taste, and stir. Serve hot or at room temperature.

Serves 4 or more

Divine

The Best Green Beans with Bacon

Roasting green beans at a high temperature makes them all wrinkled and very delicious.

1 pound green beans, ends trimmed
1 tablespoon olive oil
4 slices of bacon

1. Preheat the oven to 400 degrees.

2. Wash the beans and dry. Toss with the olive oil and sprinkle with salt. Put the beans in one layer on a rimmed baking sheet. Bake for 20 minutes, shaking the pan once or twice during this time to prevent sticking.

3. Meanwhile, cook the bacon in a skillet over medium-high heat until just crispy. Drain on paper towels. Chop into small pieces.

4. After about 20 minutes, the green beans will be wrinkled and have golden-brown spots. Transfer to a large bowl or platter and sprinkle with salt and freshly ground black pepper. Toss well and scatter the bacon on top. Serve hot or at room temperature.

Serves 4

Roasted Rosemary
Potatoes

Rosemary is a potato's best friend.

1½ pounds Yukon Gold potatoes
1 tablespoon finely chopped fresh rosemary
2½ tablespoons olive oil

1. Preheat the oven to 400 degrees.

2. Peel the potatoes and cut them into 1-inch chunks. Put them in a bowl. Add the rosemary, 2 tablespoons of the olive oil, and 2 teaspoons salt. Stir well to coat the potatoes thoroughly.

3. Drizzle the remaining ½ tablespoon of olive oil on a rimmed baking sheet. Bake for 35 minutes, turning the potatoes with a spatula every 10 minutes. When the potatoes are crispy and tender, transfer them to a large plate. Sprinkle with salt.

Serves 4

Creamy Potato Gratin

You will feel like a great French chef when you make this classic recipe.

4 ounces Gruyere or Comté cheese
4 baking potatoes, about 2 pounds
1½ cups half-and-half

1. Preheat the oven to 350 degrees.

2. Shred the cheese on the large holes of a box grater. You will have about 1 packed cup. Set aside.

3. Peel the potatoes and cut across the width into very thin slices. Spray an 8 x 8-inch glass baking dish or a small shallow casserole with cooking spray. Arrange one third of the slices, overlapping, in the bottom of the dish. Sprinkle with ¼ teaspoon salt and freshly ground black pepper. Cover with one third of the cheese. Make 2 more layers of potatoes and cheese, sprinkling each layer with ¼ teaspoon salt and freshly ground black pepper.

4. Pour the half-and-half over the top. Bake for 25 minutes and press the potatoes down firmly with a spatula. Cook for 25 minutes longer, until golden brown.

Serves 6

Mashed Potato

Add-Ons

Bacon bits

Blue cheese crumbles

Buttermilk

Chopped fresh herbs

Chopped scallions

Corn kernels

Creamed spinach

Crispy onions

Gravy

Peas

Pesto sauce

Roasted garlic

Sautéed mushrooms

Sautéed onions

Shredded cheddar cheese

Sour cream

Sun-dried tomatoes

Wasabi paste

The Best Mashed Potatoes

The best mashed potatoes are made with baking potatoes to which hot milk and cold butter are added. Yum!

5 large baking potatoes, about 2 pounds

1 cup milk

6 tablespoons (¾ stick) unsalted butter

1. Peel the potatoes. Cut in half lengthwise and then crosswise. Place in a medium pot with water to cover by 1 inch. Add 1 tablespoon of salt and bring to a rapid boil. Cover the pot and cook over medium heat for 25 minutes, or until the potatoes are tender. Remove the potatoes from the pot with a slotted spoon and place them in a colander in the sink. Pat dry and put them in a large bowl.

2. Put the milk in a small saucepan and bring just to a boil. Lower the heat and cook for 1 minute.

3. Using a potato masher, mash the potatoes, slowly adding the hot milk. Add small bits of butter and continue to mash until they reach the desired consistency. Some folks like them lumpy; others like them smooth. Add salt and freshly ground black pepper to taste.

Serves 6 (makes 5 cups)

Marvelous mashed potatoes
make a meal memorable!

Sweet Potato Wedges with Maple Syrup

This is an unexpectedly delicious treat for a party.

2 large sweet potatoes, 8 ounces each
2 tablespoons vegetable oil
¼ cup real maple syrup

1. Preheat the oven to 375 degrees.

2. Peel the sweet potatoes using a vegetable peeler. Cut each into 8 long wedges. The best way to do this is to cut the potatoes in half lengthwise and then cut each half into 4 long wedges.

3. Put the sweet potatoes in a bowl. Add the oil and toss until the potatoes are coated with oil. Place them on a rimmed baking sheet with the pointed side up.

4. Roast for 15 minutes, then turn the potatoes on another side. Bake for 8 minutes longer and turn the potatoes on their third side. Bake for about 7 minutes longer. The potatoes should be tender when pierced with a sharp knife. Total cooking time is about 30 minutes. Transfer the potatoes to a platter. Sprinkle with salt and freshly ground black pepper and drizzle with the maple syrup.

Serves 4

Creative Coconut Rice

The first two ingredients are fragrant basmati rice and light coconut milk. The third ingredient is up to you! Each one takes your taste buds in a new direction. Try them all and tell me which one you like best!

1 cup basmati rice

1 cup light coconut milk

with...

1 tablespoon unsalted butter

or...

3 tablespoons sweetened coconut

or...

⅓ cup finely chopped pistachios

or...

½ teaspoon curry powder, or more to taste

1. Put the rice, coconut milk, 1 cup water, and 1 teaspoon salt in a large saucepan with a cover. Bring to a boil, stirring once. Reduce the heat to very low, cover the saucepan, and simmer for 18 minutes, stirring once or twice during cooking. Remove from the heat and let stand covered for 5 minutes, or until all the liquid is absorbed.

2. Prepare the third ingredient. If using coconut, put the sweetened coconut in a small nonstick skillet and, stirring constantly, cook over medium-high heat, about 1 minute, until the coconut gets lightly browned. If using pistachios, toast them lightly the same way.

3. Add the butter *or* toasted coconut *or* pistachios *or* curry powder to the hot rice. Add salt and freshly ground white pepper to taste. Stir and serve.

Serves 4 or more

Dessert Menu

Heavenly Chocolate Mousse Cake

The name of the cake says it all! It is warm, rich, moist, and flourless.

16 ounces semisweet chocolate
10 tablespoons (1¼ sticks) unsalted butter
5 extra-large eggs

1. Preheat the oven to 375 degrees.

2. Line the bottom of an 8-inch springform pan with a round of parchment paper or aluminum foil. Spray the inside of the pan with cooking spray.

3. Chop the chocolate into pieces, if necessary. Cut the butter into small chunks. Place the chocolate and butter in the top of a double boiler or in a bowl over a pot of simmering water. Heat, stirring constantly, until the chocolate has melted and the mixture is smooth. Let cool.

4. Using an electric mixer, beat the eggs with a pinch of salt. Beat at high speed until the mixture is very thick and increases in volume, about 5 minutes. Slowly pour the chocolate mixture into the beaten eggs and mix gently until the chocolate is thoroughly incorporated. Pour the mixture into the prepared pan. Bake for 22 minutes.

5. Remove from the oven. The center will still be soft. Let cool for at least 45 minutes. (You can refrigerate the cake up to 2 days; let it sit at room temperature for several hours before serving.)

Serves 8

The name says it all...

Chocolate–Banana Terrine

This is even better than birthday cake and requires no baking! It looks like a loaf; the French call it a terrine. *Just add candles!*

5 small bananas (not baby bananas)
1 cup heavy cream
16 ounces milk or semisweet chocolate

1. Line an 8 by 4-inch loaf pan with plastic wrap so that the plastic wrap overhangs the edges by 3 inches. Place the bananas in the pan to make 2 layers, trimming the ends so that the bananas easily fit into the pan.

2. In a small saucepan, heat the cream over medium heat until hot, but not boiling. Add the chocolate and heat, stirring constantly, until the chocolate is completely melted and the mixture is smooth. Pour the chocolate mixture over the bananas. You want the chocolate to seep between the layers. Tap the pan down several times to release any air bubbles. Let cool. Loosely fold the plastic wrap over the top of the terrine. Refrigerate overnight or until the terrine is very firm.

3. Fold back the plastic wrap. Turn the pan upside down on a cutting board to unmold. Lift the pan from the terrine. Remove the plastic wrap and cut into thick slices.

Serves 8 or more

Warm
Banana Tart

According to Danielle Hartog, my eleven-year-old sous-chef, this recipe will make you feel like a pro.

1 sheet of frozen puff pastry (8¼ ounces)

½ cup apricot jam

3 ripe medium-size bananas

1. Preheat the oven to 375 degrees.

2. Thaw the pastry according to package directions. While the pastry is cold but bendable, roll it out with a rolling pin to stretch the dough ¼ inch longer and ¼ inch wider. Cut the dough into quarters so that you have 4 rectangles. Leaving a ¼-inch border on each side of each rectangle, prick the pastry (except the edges) all over with the tines of a fork.

3. In a small saucepan, put the jam and 2 tablespoons of water. Stir and melt over medium heat until the jam is melted and smooth.

4. Peel the bananas and slice thin. Arrange the bananas in a tight overlapping pattern to completely cover the pastry, but not the ¼-inch borders. Using a pastry brush, brush the warm jam over the bananas (do not let it drip on the edges of the pastry). Place the tarts on an ungreased baking sheet and bake for 25 minutes, or until golden. Lightly brush the bananas with the remaining melted jam. Let cool.

Serves 4

"I loved making the banana tarts because they looked sooo professional when they were done." —Danielle Hartog, age 11

Strawberries-in-Nightgowns

Here, melted chocolate covers big bright strawberries with a shiny chocolate coating that hardens as it sits. You can dip the dark chocolate berries into coconut flakes and the white chocolate berries into chocolate sprinkles. Or do it the other way around! Either way they are delicious and look beautiful, too!

16 to 20 large ripe strawberries, about 16 ounces
6 ounces semisweet or white chocolate chips
⅓ cup chocolate sprinkles or flaked coconut

1. Wash the strawberries and pat completely dry. This is an important step. Leave the green stems on for easy dipping.

2. Put the semisweet or white chocolate chips in the top of a double boiler or in a bowl over a pot of simmering water. Let the chocolate slowly melt until it is completely smooth, stirring occasionally. Remove from the heat.

3. One by one, dip each strawberry into the mixture. Cover each berry with a thin coating three-quarters of the way up and shake off any excess. You want to leave a band of the red berry showing at the top. Let them dry for 1 minute.

4. Line a large plate with waxed paper. Put sprinkles or coconut in a shallow bowl. Dip each berry in the sprinkles or coconut to lightly coat. Place on the waxed paper. Let the chocolate cool and harden. It is best to eat these the same day they are made.

> "Strawberries-in-Nightgowns were my favorite. My younger brother Daniel said they were awesome. I even tried dipping slices of clementine oranges in the chocolate mixture and called them Tangy Tops. They were delicious."
>
> *–Rachel Greenberg, age 12*

Makes 16-20

Strawberries with Mint Sugar

You will love the big, bright flavors of ripe red strawberries under a blanket of green-flecked snow. Think of other ways to use this mint-flavored sugar. I like it sprinkled on grapefruit, or you might add it to a glass of iced tea.

2 pints ripe strawberries
⅓ cup sugar
1 bunch of fresh mint

1. Wash the berries and dry well. Remove the green stems. Cut the berries in half lengthwise and place in a pretty bowl.

2. Put the sugar in the bowl of a food processor. Wash the mint and dry very well. Make sure there is absolutely no water on the mint. Remove all the mint leaves. Using a knife on a cutting board, coarsely chop enough mint leaves to get ¼ cup. Add to the sugar and process until the mint is incorporated into the sugar.

3. Sprinkle the mint sugar all over the berries and serve immediately. Garnish with a few whole leaves of remaining mint.

Serves 4

One should never turn down
the chance to make fondue!

Fresh Cherries with Chocolate Fondue

Fresh cherries are the ideal fruit for this recipe because they come with stems for easy dipping and pair especially well with chocolate. You may use chocolate chips, chunks, or bars.

1 pound fresh red cherries with stems

¾ cup light coconut milk

6 ounces semisweet chocolate, chopped in small pieces if using a bar

1. Wash the cherries and dry with a paper towel. Do not remove the stems. Chill until ready to serve.

2. Put the coconut milk in a small, heavy saucepan. Cook over medium heat until hot. Add the chocolate to the hot coconut milk. Reduce the heat to low and cook, stirring constantly, until the chocolate melts and the mixture is very smooth.

3. Transfer the mixture to a small fondue pot or a soufflé dish. Serve with the cherries for dipping.

Serves 4

This fondue is also fabulous with other food:

- Fresh orange segments, banana chunks, or wedges of apple or pear

- Lady fingers, pound cake, sugar cookies, shortbread, or biscotti

Chocolate Sandwich Cookies

Be sure to use self-rising cake flour for these brownielike cookies.

1 cup Nutella

1 extra-large egg

1¼ cups self-rising cake flour

1. Preheat the oven to 375 degrees.

2. In the bowl of an electric mixer, put ½ cup of the Nutella and the egg. Mix well. Slowly add 1 cup of the flour until a wet dough is formed. Dust a clean board or countertop with the remaining ¼ cup of flour and transfer the dough to the board. Knead gently until a smooth dough forms; the dough will be a little sticky. Roll the dough into 18 balls, flouring your hands as you go to make rolling easier. Place the balls on a parchment-lined baking sheet, several inches apart.

3. Bake for 10 to 12 minutes and remove from the oven. Let cool for 10 minutes. Using a serrated knife, cut the cookies in half horizontally. Spread the bottom with 1 teaspoon of the remaining Nutella and replace the top, pressing firmly. Let cool. Store in a tightly covered tin.

Makes 18

Simple Butter Cookies

These belong in cookie jars everywhere. They are buttery and very tender.

**1 cup (2 sticks) unsalted butter,
at room temperature**

1 cup confectioners' sugar, plus more for dusting

**2 cups all-purpose flour,
plus more for dusting the board**

1. Preheat the oven to 300 degrees.

2. Put the butter in the bowl of an electric mixer. Beat the butter until light and fluffy. You may also use a hand-held mixer. Add the sugar gradually, and beat well. Stir in the flour and add a large pinch of salt. Continue to mix on low until a smooth ball of dough is formed.

3. Sprinkle the counter or a large board lightly with flour. Using a rolling pin, roll out the dough about ¼ inch thick. Cut out the cookies using any decorative cookie cutter you desire: I like to use 2-inch-round fluted cookie cutters. Or cut out the numbers 1-2-3 using number cookie cutters; or make stars or half-moon shapes.

4. Bake on an ungreased baking sheet for about 25 minutes, or until the cookies are dry and pale in color. Remove from the baking sheet only when the cookies have cooled. Dust the cookies with additional confectioners' sugar shaken through a coarse-mesh sieve.

Makes 36 to 40 cookies

Iced Strawberry Tea

This will become one of your favorite thirst-quenchers. Great for a tea party, serve this fabulous iced tea with a big plate of Simple Butter Cookies.

**16 ounces strawberries,
plus more for garnish**

½ cup sugar

2 orange pekoe tea bags

1. Wash the berries and remove the stems. Cut the berries in half, put in the bowl of a food processor with the sugar, and process until very smooth. You will have 2 cups of purée.

2. Bring 5 cups of water to a boil. Pour the water into a large heat-proof jar, add the tea bags, and let steep for 5 minutes. Combine the berry purée with the tea. Strain through a coarse-mesh strainer into a pitcher. Let cool. Cover and refrigerate until very cold.

3. Serve over ice with additional berries as a garnish.

Serves 6

Let the nighttime oven
do its magic.

Cookies While You Sleep

*Put glossy heaps of wet meringue into the oven before bedtime
and in the morning you will wake up to dreamy crisp cookies.*

3 extra-large egg whites

⅛ cup sugar

1 heaping cup miniature chocolate chips

1. Preheat the oven to 375 degrees.

2. Beat the egg whites in the bowl of an electric mixer until
   they just begin to thicken. Add a pinch of salt and gradually
   add the sugar. Beat for several minutes, until the mixture
   holds its shape and is stiff and glossy. The mixture should
   look like Marshmallow Fluff.

3. Line 2 rimmed baking sheets with parchment paper.
   Gently fold the chocolate chips into the meringue mixture
   and drop by the tablespoonful onto the baking sheets.
   Place in the oven on the middle rack and turn the oven off
   immediately. Leave the door closed until morning.
   Sweet dreams.

Makes about 28

"For the Chocolate–Pecan Fudge we bought prechopped pecans and that saved time. We had half a can of the condensed milk left, so we just doubled the recipe and made a bigger batch. It was fantastic."

–Ben Deem, age 10

Chocolate–Pecan Fudge

This is a great little candy you can whip up easily. Great for kids and adults, too.

1 cup coarsely chopped pecans
1⅓ cups sweetened condensed milk
12 ounces semisweet chocolate chips

1. Place the pecans in a small nonstick skillet and add a large pinch of salt. Cook over medium heat, stirring constantly, until the nuts are toasted. Set aside to cool.

2. Put the condensed milk in a small saucepan. Heat until it just comes to a boil. Add the chocolate and immediately reduce the heat to low. Continue to cook, stirring constantly, until the chocolate has melted and the mixture is smooth. Stir in the pecans until well blended.

3. Line an 8 by 8-inch square pan with plastic wrap so that 4 inches hang over the sides of the pan. Pour the mixture into the pan and cover with the panels of plastic wrap. Refrigerate until cold. Cut into small squares. Let sit at room temperature for 20 minutes before serving.

Makes 16 pieces

Lemon–Buttermilk Sorbet

This is awesome: It's creamy, lemony, and sweet. Delicious on top of a mound of berries!

2 cups sugar

4 large lemons

1 quart buttermilk

1. Put the sugar in a large bowl. Wash the lemons and dry them. Grate the zest of 3 lemons and add to the sugar. Cut all the lemons in half and squeeze to get ½ cup juice. Add the juice to the sugar and stir with a wooden spoon until the mixture is smooth.

2. Whisk in the buttermilk and a pinch of salt. Stir until sugar is dissolved. Cover and chill several hours or overnight.

3. Freeze in an ice cream maker according to the manufacturer's directions.

Serves 8

Orange Sundae

This dessert—freshly made orange ice cream with orange–caramel sauce—looks especially nice when served in a big scooped-out orange instead of a bowl.

1½ cups half-and-half

1 cup sugar

3½ cups freshly squeezed orange juice

1. Put the half-and-half in a large saucepan with ¾ cup of the sugar and a pinch of salt. Bring just to a boil, whisking constantly. Remove from the heat and let cool. Add 3 cups of the orange juice to the mixture and whisk until blended. Cover and refrigerate until very cold. Freeze in an ice cream maker according to the manufacturer's directions.

2. Make orange–caramel sauce: Put the remaining ¼ cup of sugar in a small nonstick skillet. Cook over medium-high heat, stirring constantly with a wooden spoon, until the sugar turns into a dark clear liquid. With the help of an adult, carefully add the remaining ½ cup of orange juice; remember, this is very hot. The mixture will bubble up and harden, but continue to cook it over high heat until the hardened sugar melts. **(Be sure to do this step with an adult.)** Continue to cook until the sauce is reduced to 6 tablespoons. Let cool.

3. Serve the ice cream in dessert dishes or in big scooped-out oranges. Pour the sauce on top.

Serves 4

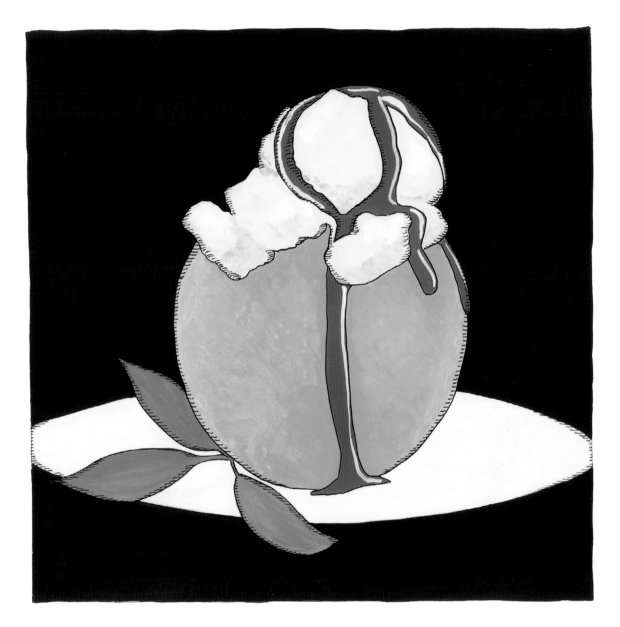

Amaze your friends and family
(no one has to know how simple it was!)

Watermelon Ices with Chocolate "Seeds"

The riper the watermelon, the more delicious this tastes. Watermelon and chocolate taste great together.

4 cups diced ripe watermelon
¾ cup sugar
½ cup miniature chocolate chips

1. Remove the seeds from the watermelon. Put the watermelon in the bowl of a food processor and process until very smooth. Add the sugar and a pinch of salt and continue to process until the sugar is dissolved.

2. Transfer the mixture to a metal pie pan and place in the freezer. After 30 minutes, break up the ice crystals with a fork so that they are of uniform size. Continue to break up ice crystals every hour until the mixture is frozen, about 3 hours.

3. When ready to serve, chill the bowl and blade of a food processor. Break the frozen mixture into chunks and place in the chilled bowl. Process until very smooth. Spoon the ices into chilled glasses or dessert dishes and sprinkle with chocolate chips. Serve immediately.

Serves 4

Quick Ice Cream Sauces...

made from ice cream!

Hot Fudge

When cold, this makes a great icing for cupcakes. When hot, it turns a simple scoop of ice cream into something special.

¾ cup vanilla ice cream
8 ounces chocolate chips
2 tablespoons light corn syrup

Put the ice cream in a small, heavy saucepan over medium heat. Let it melt and then bring just to a boil. Add the chocolate, then immediately lower the heat. Stir constantly until the sauce is smooth. Add the corn syrup and cook for 1 minute, stirring constantly. Serve immediately or reheat before ready to serve.

Makes 1¼ cups

Maple–Walnut Sauce

Sous-chef Ben Deem didn't think he would like this at all, but after making it, he thought it was fabulous!

6 tablespoons real maple syrup
½ cup vanilla ice cream
⅓ cup chopped walnuts

Put the maple syrup and a pinch of salt in a small saucepan. Bring to a boil, then lower the heat to medium. Continue to cook, not stirring, until the syrup reduces a little and thickens, about 5 minutes. Using a wire whisk, whisk in the ice cream until completely smooth, cooking 1 minute longer. Remove from the heat and stir in the walnuts. Serve immediately or reheat gently before serving.

Makes about ½ cup

"The hot fudge was really easy to make. It was like the really gooey warm fudge you'd find in an ice cream shop."

–Ben Deem, age 10

Index